"What Are You Doin' in There?"
A Bathroom Companion (for Kids!)

by The Editors of
Planet Dexter

A Satellite of Addison Wesley Longman

ISBN 0-201-95990-9

Copyright © 1996 by The Editors of Planet Dexter

1 2 3 4 5 6 7 8 9-RNT-0099989796

First printing, September 1996

Through the Addison Wesley Longman TRIΔNGLE Program, Planet Dexter books are available FROM YOUR BOOKSELLER at special discounts for bulk purchases; or contact the Corporate, Government, and Special Sales Department at Addison Wesley Longman, One Jacob Way, Reading, MA 01867, or call (800) 238-9682.

Who Did This?!?

Compiled by **Jess Brallier**

Edited by **Beth Wolfensberger Singer**

General Confusion by **Michael Cirone**

Cover design by **C. Shane Sykes**

Safety Net by **Susan Howard**

Cover Art by **Jack Keely**

Interior Insanity by **MKR Design, Inc.**

Set in **so many fonts we couldn't count them all.**

Illustrations © 1996 by:
Joe Bartos
Jim Paillot
Randy Verougstraete

Electronic art by **Rachel Geswaldo**

Eye Candy for the Bathroom
A Table of Contents

BILLY

*a*ll through your life, people are going to tell you that reading is a good thing to do. People will tell you what you "should" read, and they'll tell you when you should read it. But will they tell you where to read it?

Not likely.

The bedroom is an excellent place to read, and so is the kitchen. The front porch, a lawn, the basement: all these locations have their merits. But bathroom reading can be the most satisfying reading you do. Why? Because, if you read there, you're usually accomplishing two things at once. Very efficient. If you know what we mean.

You should be warned that this book comes from Planet Dexter. We do a lot of stuff on Planet Dexter. One of the things we do is publish books we hope will help introduce kids to the world in which they live. Kids live a lot of their lives in the bathroom. So it's only logical that we couldn't resist putting together this book, and giving it a name that, at some point, every person who is a devoted bathroom reader is bound to hear from a parent or sibling knocking at the bathroom door.

"Whaddaya Doin' in There????"

What are *you going to be doing in there?* Well, hang onto your (toilet) seats, because this book is brimming with readable wonders that'll keep you amused and informed while you pass ... time in the most interesting room in the house.

Answer: Absolutely! Here's Why.

Important Note: Someday we'd like to publish another Bathroom Companion, one packed full of great stuff that you readers have supplied. *Seriously.* If you've got some good stuff—trivia, jokes, mind teasers, quotes, whatever!—that you think might be appropriate, send it to us at:

**The Editors of Planet Dexter
One Jacob Way
Reading, MA 01867-3999**

Or fax us at (617) 944-8243; or e-mail us via the Internet at pdexter@aw.com, or via America Online at PDexter.

We sure do hope you enjoy this book; and remember, once you're on the toilet, it's not healthy to rush things.

So read on.

The Editors of Planet Dexter

And N☺W a Message from Our Corporate Lawyer:

"Neither the Publisher nor the Author shall be liable for any damage that may be caused or sustained as a result of conducting any of the activities in this book without specifically following instructions, conducting the activities without proper supervision, or ignoring the cautions contained in the book."

Benjamin Franklin is said to have owned America's first bathtub, in which he did much of his reading and letter-writing.

A Little Bathroom History

"I need to go to the bathroom!"

Sure, you can say that *now*. But consider yourself lucky that you live in modern times. The bathroom wasn't even invented until about 10,000 years ago, when someone on Orkney, an island near Scotland, set up the first such room and gave it a drainage system that sent bodily waste to a local stream. There you had it: the state-of-the-art bathroom of 8,000 B.C.

Togetherness

Much later but still a very long time ago, the ancient Romans built extremely fancy public bathrooms, where both men and women could bathe. No "Women's" and "Men's" doors there.

A Royal Flush

If you were in France during the late 1600s and got an invitation to come meet King Louis XIV while he sat on his toilet, would you accept the invite? Some people of that time did, and thought it was a great honor to visit with the king on the potty.

Public Restrooms

Until the early 1800s, Europeans pooped and peed either in chamber pots (bowls, basically, kept in people's houses), in outhouses, or on the very streets of their towns and cities. Imagine what it would be like to run into one of your friends, your teachers, or your neighbors going to the bathroom in the street. The Europeans of the 1800s had to deal with this problem often.

There wasn't any way to "flush" the chamber pots of that time — someone had to empty them out. Usually there was a kind of garbage man who would do the job. But sometimes the pots got full before the garbage man arrived, so people just threw the stuff in the pots out their windows. All the germs caused by this dumping made it easy for horrible diseases to spread through the cities.

Birth of the Toilet

Every time you marvel at how the toilet can whoosh your bodily stuff away, you can thank Alexander Cumming for it. He was an English guy who, in 1775, invented the first toilet that didn't smell bad. How did he do it? He put a bend in one of the pipes (see "Toilet Anatomy," pages 14 and 15), which caused the pipe to hold water at all times. The water blocked the smell. Hooray!

And the Birth of **tp**

Back before there was toilet paper, people used leaves, corn cobs, even their hands when necessary. Many American folks used pages of the Sears Catalog. But in 1880 the Scott brothers (sound familiar?) finally made what we would recognize as toilet paper. They were pretty happy about their invention because they knew that people would always need more of it.

The Greek scientist Archimedes was soaking in his bathtub when he came up with an important law of physics. He noticed that a body (in this case, his body) set into fluid, (in this case, his bathwater) loses weight equal to the weight of the fluid the body displaces. He was so hyped up about his discovery that he jumped out of the tub and ran into the streets naked, yelling **"Eureka!,"** which means "I have found it!"

Weird —BUT REAL!— Laws

☛ You may not move your bed in Huntsville, Alabama without first getting a permit from the police.

☛ In Birmingham, Alabama, it's illegal to put a blindfold on and then drive your car.

☛ The following dances are illegal in Iowa City's public dance halls: the Turkey Trot, the Grizzly Bear, the Charleston, the Texas Tommy, and the Bunny Hug.

☛ In Topeka, Kansas, it's against the law to wheel someone around in a wheelbarrow.

☛ In Lewes, Delaware, men are forbidden from wearing pants with snug waists.

☛ In Louisiana, robbers cannot under any circumstances shoot at bank tellers with water pistols.

☛ No one is allowed to cross the street by walking on his or her hands in Hartford, Connecticut.

☛ In Greene, New York, you cannot walk backwards and eat peanuts on the sidewalks during a concert.

☛ It's illegal in Salem, West Virginia, to leave your home without knowing where you're going.

☛ In Natoma, Kansas, no one is allowed to throw knives at men in striped suits.

- In Michigan, it's illegal to place a skunk inside the desk of your boss.

- It's forbidden in Oneida, Tennessee, for anyone to sing the song "It Ain't Goin' To Rain No Mo'."

- In Tulsa, Oklahoma, no man can walk around in public with his shirt untucked.

- It's against the law to whistle while under water in Vermont.

- In Leahy, Washington, it's against the law to blow your nose while on the streets, because you might frighten a horse.

- In 1934, the Kentucky state legislature passed a Nudist Colony Bill that required regular inspection of the nudists by members of the Kentucky state legislature.

- Nicholas County, West Virginia, forbids clergy to crack jokes from the pulpit.

- In Blue Earth, Minnesota, no child under age 12 can chat on the phone unless a parent is present in the room.

- In Stockton, California, it's illegal to "wiggle" while dancing.

An automatic spaghetti-spinning fork was patented in 1950.

"People think that I must be a very strange person. This is not correct. I have the heart of a small boy. It is in a glass jar on my desk."
  —Stephen King

"The highlight of my childhood was making my brother laugh so hard that food came out of his nose."
  —Garrison Keillor

"People who get nostalgic about childhood were obviously never children."
  —Bill Watterson, creator of Calvin and Hobbes

"Do you know why grown-ups are always asking little kids what they want to be when they grow up? It's because they're looking for ideas."
  —Paula Poundstone

"When you are eight years old, nothing is any of your business."
  —Lenny Bruce

"I was so naive as a kid I used to sneak behind the barn and do nothing."
  —Johnny Carson

"When I was growing up I always wanted to be someone. Now I realize I should have been more specific."
  —Lily Tomlin

"When I was kidnapped my parents snapped into action. They rented my room."
  —Woody Allen

King George II of England **fell** *to* **his death** from a toilet seat.

In China, a Coca-Cola advertisement used Chinese characters to sound out "Coca-Cola." The advertisement was quickly dropped after it was learned that the characters meant **"Bite the wax tadpole."**

How come phonetic isn't spelled the way it sounds?

Would Adam or Eve have had a bellybutton?

Have you ever imagined what life would be like if there were no hypothetical situations?

Whenever a plane crashes, the indestructible "little black box" is always found intact. Why don't plane makers simply make the whole plane out of whatever they use to make the box?

Why are there interstate highways in Hawaii?

How come a "perm" (short for "permanent wave") grows out?

Has this sentence ever been used: "Hey, hand me that grand piano."

If 7-Elevens are open all day and night, every day of the year, why do they bother installing locks on their doors?

If nothing ever sticks to TEFLON, how do manufacturers get TEFLON to stick to the surface of a frying pan?

Why do they put Braille dots on the keypad of the drive-up ATM?

Why do we drive on parkways and park on driveways?

If "instant replay" were really "instant," would the announcer have time to call it an "instant replay"?

Isn't "yes" the only possible answer to the question, "Are you awake?"

Toilet Anatomy

If you look at a diagram of a toilet, you will see that something is seriously wrong. Well, maybe not "wrong," but illogical. See that pipe that curves up from the toilet bowl *(the round part of the toilet that you sit on)*? Water actually flows *up* that thing when you press the handle to flush the toilet. How does that happen? Easy as **A B C**.

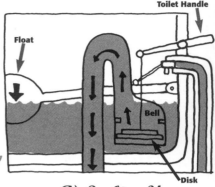

Toilet Handle

Float

Bell

Disk

a) Sucking Up

Check out the part of the diagram labeled the **DISK.** When you push the toilet's handle down, it lifts the disk up. This creates something called a siphon. A siphon is a situation in which the water pressure in a tube makes the water rise upward. The disk creates enough of a siphon so that the pressure of the water in the toilet's tank *(the square part that sits behind your back when you're sitting on the toilet)* makes the water go up the pipe.

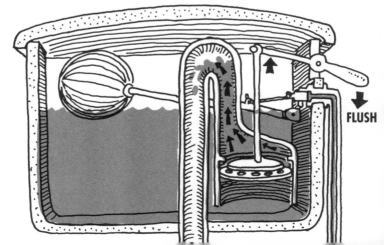

FLUSH

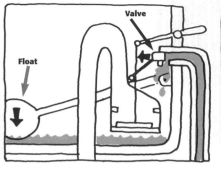

Valve

Float

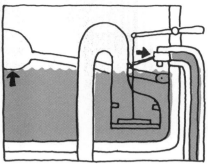

B) Slurping

You can see that the part of the diagram labeled **BELL** doesn't quite hit the bottom of the tank. So when you press the handle and the siphon makes the water in the tank flow up that pipe, enough water is drained from the tank that, in a few seconds, the water level falls below the bottom of the bell. At that point, air goes in the bell in a kind of slurpy, bubbly way, and the siphon stops working. But it doesn't matter, because the **FLOAT** (*see diagram above*) is connected up in such a way that it now hits the bottom of the tank and the other end of it pulls out that little stopper thing we call the **VALVE** (*see diagram again*).

C) Whooshing

That valve is a stopper to the pipe that supplies water to the toilet, so when the bell is low, and the stopper is pulled open, water whooshes back into the tank of the toilet, filling it up, and also putting water in the bowl. It stops filling when the float floats high enough in the tank. *Why?* Because when the float is sitting so the bar on it is level, the valve goes back into the pipe.

The National Rotten Sneaker Championship takes place in Montpelier, Vermont. People show up wearing dirty, old, and very, very, very stinky sneakers. The contest winners get a new pair of sneakers and a can of foot powder.

"WHADDAYA DOIN' IN THERE?"

First Sentences

(from Books Great and Not So Great)

Match the book title with the book's first sentence. If you fail to get the correct answers for **Old Yeller**, **The Adventures of Tom Sawyer**, and **Forrest Gump**, we strongly suggest that upon leaving the bathroom, you proceed directly to your local library.

On January 20, 1795, in the Netherlands, a company of cavalry (soldiers on horses) actually defeated and captured a fleet of ships. The French cavalry, riding around in freezing weather, discovered that the Dutch fleet was trapped in waters that had turned to ice. The horseman surrounded the Dutch ships and captured them.

Book

1. *Old Yeller*
by Fred Gipson

2. *The Adventures of Tom Sawyer*
by Mark Twain

3. *Forrest Gump*
by Winston Groom

4. *Microserfs*
by Douglas Coupland

5. *Stuart Little*
by E.B. White

6. *Catcher in the Rye*
by J.D. Salinger

7. *Gone with the Wind*
by Margaret Mitchell

8. *The Diary of a Young Girl*
by Anne Frank

9. *Get Smart: An Original Novel about Super-Spy, Maxwell Smart*
by William Johnston

First Sentence

a. This morning, just after 11:00, Michael locked himself in his office and he won't come out.

b. We called him Old Yeller.

c. Tom!

d. Let me say this: being a idiot is no box of chocolates.

e. I hope I will be able to confide everything to you, as I have never been able to confide in anyone, and I hope you will be a great source of comfort and support.

f. It was a typical spring morning in New York City.

g. When Mrs. Frederick C. Little's second son arrived, everybody noticed that he was not much bigger than a mouse.

h. Scarlett O'Hara was not beautiful, but men seldom realized it when caught by her charm.

i. If you really want to hear about it, the first thing you'll probably want to know is where I was born, and what my lousy childhood was like, and how my parents were occupied and all before they had me, and all that David Copperfield kind of crap, but I don't feel like going into it, if you want to know the truth.

Answers: 1. b; 2. c; 3. d; 4. a; 5. g; 6. i; 7. h; 8. e; 9. f.

"WHADDAYA DOIN' IN THERE?"

The Interrupted Date
(Boo!)

A boyfriend and girlfriend who rarely had any time alone together were finally able to borrow the boy's dad's car for the evening. They lived in a tiny town where there was virtually nada to do at night, so they decided to drive the car to a tree-lined road at the edge of town, sit together in the front seat, and talk. And, of course, kiss.

The boyfriend had had to clean his room before he was allowed to borrow the car that night, so by the time they parked, it was already very dark out. The boyfriend, noticing how late it was already, wanted to skip all the talking and start making out. He turned on the radio in search of some romantic music. But the first thing he heard was a news broadcast.

"Important announcement," the man on the radio said. "Please take extra care if you are on the roads tonight. A convicted killer has escaped from our local mental hospital, and he is known to be traveling with a stolen carving knife."

The boyfriend tried to switch the station, but the girlfriend stopped him.

"The killer can be easily identified, as he is missing his right hand, and wears a hook in place of it," the radio announcer said.

"Anyone with information about the whereabouts of the killer should call the police immediately."

"Wow," said the girlfriend. "Think we should go home?"

The boyfriend laughed. "We're safe out here," he said. "Look, I'll lock the doors." And he did. He tuned the radio to a station playing a slow song, and put his arm around the girlfriend's shoulder, but she pulled away.

"I'm nervous," she said. "I don't like the sound of that: a killer with a knife. And here we are on a road where there's no one to help us if anything happened. What if we ran out of gas? If the guy has a hook on his hand, he can break right through the window, no matter if the doors are locked or not."

"I'd protect you," said the boyfriend, who had his other arm around her by now, and was whispering in her ear.

"Yeah, right," the girlfriend said, rolling her eyes. She elbowed him away. "Listen. Just take me home. Right now. I'm not in the mood for this."

The boyfriend was offended, but he wasn't about to sit around making a fool of himself. He put the key in the ignition and turned it so quickly that the car seemed to scream.

Or something seemed to.

"What was that?" gasped the girlfriend.

But the boyfriend was so mad at her that he didn't answer. He stomped on the gas petal and the cark jerked forward so hard that the girl had to grasp the dashboard. "What are you doing?" she asked him. "You're ticked off at me, aren't you?"

He just kept driving, much faster than he should, without saying a thing.

Soon, though, he noticed that she was crying. "I'm sorry," she said. "I was really scared. Aren't you?" He put his arm around her, suddenly feeling brave and protective.

"I'm not scared of *anything*," he said. "You just stick with me."

When he pulled up in front of the girlfriend's house, she had stopped crying, and was smiling at him a little. He remembered that she liked it when he got out

of his side of the car and came around to open her door for her, so he decided to do that. But when he got to her door, he just stood there looking at it, frozen in place.

The girlfriend noticed him standing there staring at the door. It was still locked, so she figured he was waiting for her to unlock it. She unlocked it, but he remained standing there, his eyes wide and the color drained from his face.

"What is it?" she asked, suddenly becoming alarmed herself. She pulled the door's handle and popped it open.

"Don't!" cried the boy. And as she started to get out of the car she finally saw what he was looking at. There was a long splatter of bright red blood leading from the back bumper of the car all the way up to the outside handle on her door.

And swinging there on the handle was a metal hook.

President Woodrow Wilson couldn't read until he was 11 years old.

19

The Invention of Toys
Hits and Flops

The Frisbee — Hit!

In the mid-1940s, students at Yale University began tossing around empty pie tins inscribed with the name of the pie's baker: William Russell Frisbie.

When, in the late 1950s, the Wham-O Manufacturing Company began preliminary introduction of its plastic *"Flyin' Saucer"* toy to students at Yale, Wham-O discovered students already playing with "Frisbies." Wham-O liked that name better, changed the spelling, and soon launched a national craze.

Instant Fish — Flop!

What would you do if you learned that there's a kind of fish whose eggs could sit around forever if kept dry, but only grew into fish when exposed to water?

One of the owners of the Wham-O Manufacturing Company (which brought the world the Hula Hoop, not to mention Frisbees) heard of just such a thing. This was back in the early 1960s. The fish eggs, to him, sounded like the ideal toy. Just add water and you've got instant pets! He decided to call them "Instant Fish."

Everyone back at his office was crazy about the idea, and when he showed the idea to toy store owners, they wanted to buy the "Instant Fish" right away. So many toy store owners wanted to carry "Instant Fish" that Wham-O started getting nervous, and announced that it wouldn't take any more orders. But the toy store owners snuck even more order forms to Wham-O, so excited were they about all the money to be made by selling this hot new toy.

The people at Wham-O were thrilled — for awhile. But it turned out that the fish they'd brought in to their plant were unable to lay the "Instant Fish" eggs fast enough to supply the toy store owners. What to do? They tried cooling the rooms in which the fish were kept, and when that didn't work, they tried warming them up. They covered their windows to give the fish a darker envirnoment. They even played romantic music for the fish. **But no dice**. The fish wouldn't lay the eggs any faster.

Eventually, Whamo-O gave up, canceling all of its "Instant Fish" orders. The fish had flopped big time, which is why your folks never got to play with them.

"Wow! Cool!" thought The Editors of Planet Dexter when they read about Wham-O's "Instant Fish" flop. Let's try that again but not mess it up! Let's put some instant, just-add-water eggs of some sort with a fun book. And let's make sure we have enough of them!

That challenge led us—seriously!—through Harvard University, Brown University, The New England Aquarium, Carolina Biological Supply, and at last, to Dr. Eugene Hull, an inventor, embryologist, and breeder of what he calls "Triops" (from the Greek word for "three eyes").

Instead of Triops, we decided to call them "Instant Creatures." And the book-with-eggs-and-food we called ***Instant Creature! The Swimming Critters from Way Back Then***. The book soon went on to be one of the most popular titles on Planet Dexter.

Hit! **Wiffle Ball**

Holey Moses! How did the Wiffle Ball get it's holes?

Well, a man named David Mullaney thought it up. Actually, it was his son who inspired the Wiffle Ball. The son and a friend liked to play stickball using one of Mullaney's plastic golf balls. Mullaney thought about that, realized that there was something to be said for a ball that didn't roll or bounce as far as a rubber ball, and then started experimenting. He cut holes into one of his golf balls and played with it. Soon he noticed that if you put the holes in the right place, even the wimpiest thrower could toss that thing around like a pro.

So in 1955, Mullaney started making and selling Wiffle Balls (the name from the baseball term "to whiff," which means to strike out). Needless to say, it became a classic toy. Let's hope he thanked his son.

A "zarf" is a holder for a handleless coffee cup.

"The first digital computer, of course, was a set of ten fingers that somebody realized could be used for counting."
—Gene DeWeese, 1984

"I think there is a world market for about five computers."
—Thomas J. Watson, Chairman of IBM, 1943

"Why does it take a computer magazine six to eight weeks to change your address when you move? Don't they use computers?"
—John McCormick, 1990

"It means you can try to answer questions you thought the universe was going to have to do without."
—Bruce Knapp, on super-computers, 1984

"For every computer error, there are at least two human errors, one of which is blaming it on the computer."
—Joel Makower, 1984

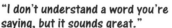

"I don't understand a word you're saying, but it sounds great."
— television executive Mr. Azae to computer designer Richard Dumner in the great Spencer Tracy/ Katherine Hepburn movie *Desk Set*, 1957

"Who has such a large Christmas card mailing list that you need to keep it on a computer? If so, why aren't I on it?"
— David D. Thornburg, 1985

"There is no reason for any individual to have a computer in their home."
— Ken Olson, President of Digital Equipment Corporation, 1977

"Software is what makes your computer behave and look smarter than it is."
— Winn Schwartau, 1994

"From then on, when anything went wrong with a computer, we said it had bugs in it."
— Grace Murray Hopper, on the removal of a two-inch-long moth from an experimental computer at Harvard in 1945

"Computers are useless. They can only give you answers."
— Pablo Picasso (1881–1973)

Rice paper has no rice in it.

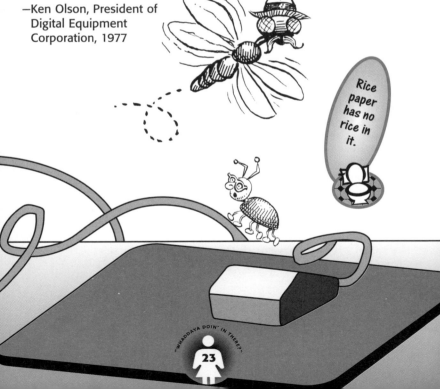

"Hollywood is a place where people from Iowa mistake each other for movie stars."
—Fred Allen

"Steven's room was a mess. Once his lizard got out of its cage, and we found it, living, three years later. He had a parakeet he refused to keep in a cage. Every week, I would stick my head in his room, grab his dirty laundry and slam the door. If I had known better, I would have taken him to a psychiatrist—and there never would have been an 'E.T.'"
—Leah Speilberg
(Steven's Mom)

"I just don't feel that my algebra teacher should ever know what my butt looks like."
—Julia Roberts, on why she won't do nude scenes

"Novelty is always welcome, but talking pictures are just a fad."
—Irving Thalberg, MGM production head in the late 1920s, on movies with sound

"I must say, it's the best bed-and-breakfast in America."
—Tom Hanks, after he and his wife stayed at the Clinton White House

"A celebrity is any well-known TV or movie star who looks like he spends more than two hours on his hair."
—Steve Martin

> **"That was my one big Hollywood hit, but, in a way, it hurt my picture career. After that, I was typecast as a lion, and there just weren't many parts for lions."**
>
> —Bert Lahr, on his role in *The Wizard of Oz*

"My movies were the kind they show in prisons and airplanes, because nobody can leave."
—Burt Reynolds, on his less successful films

"I dream for a living."
—Steven Spielberg

"I'm an actor, not a star. Stars are people who live in Hollywood and have heart-shaped pools."
—Al Pacino

"An actor's a guy who, if you ain't talking about him, ain't listening."
—Marlon Brando

Sea gulls have a red dot on their beaks. When a baby gull is hungry, it pecks on the red dot on its parent's beak. This causes the parent to open its mouth and puke out the young's dinner.

Dear Editors of
Planet Dexter,

Why do women hold their knees together, make funny faces, and stand in line?

Sincerely,
"Just Curious"
(from Lima, Ohio)

Dear Curious,

You're a guy, right? Even so, you've probably noticed a long line at the women's rest room where there is no line at the men's rest room. A group of college students conducted a study to find out why. Men average about forty-five seconds to use the toilet, while women spend about seventy-nine seconds. The extra seconds add to a long wait.

Hope that helps.

Sincerely,
The Editors of Planet Dexter

Dear Planet Dexter

(the Freezing Eyeball)

Dear Editors of Planet Dexter,

When I'm watching T.V. and see those explorers in the Antarctic and they're all covered with top-notch insulated clothing from toe to head, from ear to ear, all over, how come their eyes aren't covered and why don't their eyeballs freeze?

Sincerely,
Warm-and-cozy in front of the TV

Dear Warm-and-cozy,

The eyeballs don't become ice-balls for several reasons. Think about it: most of your eye is stuck in your head, not exposed to the air; and when you're in really cold wind, you'll tend to squint, anyway, which further reduces the amount of your eye that's out in the cold. That's one good reason. Also, when the body gets cold, it automatically sends lots of warm blood to important organs like the brain and heart and innards, so the eyeballs get heated by the blood in the brain. And lastly, remember how tears taste salty? Sodium causes that, and the sodium in your eye helps keep the water in it from freezing up.

Sincerely,
The Editors of Planet Dexter

President Andrew Jackson thought the world was flat.

"WHADDAYA DOIN' IN THERE?"

27

"It's kind of hard to rally 'round the math class."

—Bear Bryant, football coach, justifying the role of athletics in college

"This is a sport?"

—Red Smith, sportswriter, on auto racing

"You'd see guys bowling overhand."

—Rodney Dangerfield, on how tough his childhood neighborhood was

"Golf is a good walk spoiled."

—Mark Twain

"This isn't nuclear physics, it's a game. How smart do you really have to be?"

—Terry Bradshaw, quarterback, on football

"My biggest thrill came the night Elgin Baylor and I combined for 73 points in Madison Square Garden. Elgin had 71 of them."

—Hot Rod Hundley, basketball all-star-turned-broadcaster

"My family was so poor they couldn't afford any kids. The lady next door had me."

—Lee Trevino, professional golfer

"I always turn to the sports page first. The sports page records people's accomplishments; the front page has nothing but man's failures.

—Earl Warren

"Didn't come up here to read. Came up here to hit."

—Hank Aaron, on being told by manager Casey Stengel to hold the bat in such a way that its trademark would show

"Till I was 13, I thought my name was 'Shut Up.'"

—Joe Namath

"I fear Allah, thunderstorms, and bad airplane rides."

—Muhammad Ali, boxer

"Superman don't need no seat belt."

—Muhammad Ali, commenting to flight attendant, who replied, "Superman don't need no airplane, either."

French Fries were invented in Belgium.

Our Friend, the Hot Dog

During the average day in America, 50 million hot dogs will be consumed.

In 1970 at Camp David, the presidential retreat, Prince Charles and Princess Anne of the British Commonwealth feasted on barbecued hot dogs; the Royal Family's never been the same since.

The average American eats between 80 and 100 hot dogs a year.

From Memorial Day to Labor Day, Americans enjoy more than five billion hot dogs (laid end to end, that's enough to encircle the globe more than 15 times).

The favorite meal of Marlene Dietrich, the actress, was hot dogs and champagne.

In 1976, the grand eastern seaboard city of Philadelphia celebrated the American Bicentennial with the unveiling of a five-foot-long 1,776-ounce hot dog.

In 1957, the United States Chamber of Commerce officially designated July as *National Hot Dog Month*.

According to the theme song from *The Patty Duke Show*, what makes Patty lose control? You guessed it, a hot dog!

In May, 1983, a **1,983-foot-long** hot dog was made by Bill-Mar Foods of Zeeland, Wisconsin.

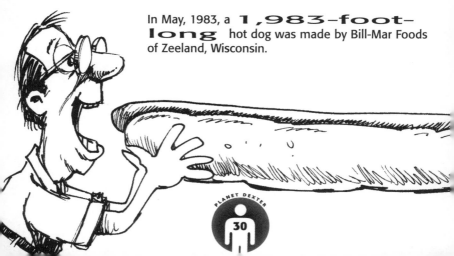

Cincinnati was so famous for its hog industry in the 1830s that it was nicknamed "Porkopolis."

In 1978, a 6-foot-long, 681-pound all-beef hot dog in a 100-pound poppy seed bun slathered with two gallons of mustard was served by David Berg of Chicago.

Babe Ruth once downed **12 hot dogs** between games of a doubleheader.

The United States Department of Agriculture officially recognizes the following as legitimate names for the hot dog: 1) wiener, 2) frankfurter, 3) frank, and 4) furter.

There are over 3,000 licensed hot dog vendors in New York City, providing 13,000 jobs (including bakers, meat packers, delivery people, and pushcart manufacturers).

Rawley's, a drive-in located in Fairfield, Connecticut, which is renowned around the world over the last 45 years for its extraordinary hot dogs, counts among its customers the very rich and the very famous—people such as Paul Newman, Dennis Quaid, Meg Ryan, Mike Wallace, Phil Simms, and Joe Namath.

"In place of the single hot dog of today there should be a variety as great as that which has come to prevail among sandwiches. There should be hot dogs for all appetites, all tastes, all occasions. They should come in rolls of every imaginable kind and be accompanied by every sort of relish, from Worcestershire sauce to chutney. The hot dog should be elevated to the level of an art form."
—H.L. Mencken, social and cultural critic, in 1929

Top 10 Ways to Stop the
Hiccups

10 Swallow hard.

9 Pull your knees up to your chest.

8 Swallow a spoonful of sugar.

7 Breathe into a brown paper bag for 20 seconds.

6 Go for a walk in the sunshine.

5 Drink a glass of water very slowly.

4 Suck on a slice of lemon.

2 Have a parent or sibling pat you gently but quickly on the upper back.

3 Ask someone to scare you.

and the
Number 1
way to Stop the Hiccups

Surprise yourself by doing all of the above at once.

One day in 1922 Charles Osborne of Iowa started hiccuping. He stopped 22 years later, after more than 400 million hiccups.

If You're not Alone . . .

While you're sitting there reading this bathroom reader, is there somebody in the shower? Or in the next stall over? If so, give this a try. (Let's pretend this other person in the bathroom is named Susan.)

Yell over and ask Susan to think of a number between 1 and 10 (but make sure Susan does *not* tell you the number!).

Then ask Susan to multiply that number by 9.

Next, instruct her to add the two digits of the answer together. (If, for example, Susan originally picked 8, after multiplying she's at the number 72; add the 7 and 2 together to get 9.)

On December 5, 1664, a ship off the coast of Wales sank with 81 passengers on board. There was one survivor, a man named Hugh Williams. On the same date in 1785, a ship sank with 60 passengers aboard. Again, there was one survivor, a man named Hugh Williams. Then, on the very same date in 1860, a ship sank with 25 passengers on board. There was one survivor—a man named Hugh Williams. This is true. And very, very weird. Now, whenever we go boating on Planet Dexter, all of us legally change our name to Hugh Williams before boarding.

At this point, Susan will be thinking of the number 9. *She has to be.* Because when anybody multiplies any number between 1 and 10 by 9, the digits of the answer always total 9. Think about it: 9, 18, 27, 36, 45, 54, 63, 72, 81, 90. Neat, eh? Now you've got Susan just where you want her.

Tell Susan to subtract 5 from the number. (You know the answer is 4 because 9 – 5 = 4.)

Tell Susan to assign a letter, according to the alphabet, to the number they end up with: a=1, b=2, c=3, d=4, e=5, and so on. (You know that the assigned letter has to be "d," right?)

Now ask Susan to think of a country in Europe that starts with that letter. (*Susan will have to think of Denmark because that's the only country in Europe that starts with "d."*)

Now ask Susan to think of an animal that starts with second letter of the country she's thinking of. (She's thinking of "e," right? And she'll most likely think of "elephant"—almost everybody does.)

We're almost there. Ask Susan to think of the color of that animal.

Now you're set to stun Susan. Ask her if she's thinking of a "gray elephant from Denmark."

Smart Advice

"A good scare is worth more to a man than good advice."
—Ed Howe

"Remember that as a teenager you are in the last stage of your life when you will be happy to hear that the phone is for you."
—Fran Lebowitz

"There are two things to aim at in life: first, to get what you want; and, after that, to enjoy it. Only the wisest of mankind achieve the second."
—Logan Pearsall Smith

"Outside of a dog, a man's best friend is a book. Inside of a dog, it's very dark."
—Groucho Marx

"Never go to a doctor whose office plants have died."
—Erma Bombeck

"To promise not to do a thing is the surest way in the world to make a body want to go and do that very thing."
—Mark Twain

"All sorrows can be borne if you tell a story about them."
—Karen Blixen

"No man has a good enough memory to be a successful liar."
—Abraham Lincoln

"Genius is one percent inspiration and ninety-nine percent perspiration."
—Thomas Alva Edison

The most popular ice cream flavor is vanilla. Chocolate comes in second, and butter pecan third.

"If you go long enough without a bath, even the fleas will let you alone."
—Ernie Pyle

"Eighty percent of success is showing up."
—Woody Allen

"It is better to know some of the questions than all of the answers."
—James Thurber

"Advice is seldom welcome. And those who want it most always like it the least."
—Phillip Dormer Stanhope

Rattlesnakes live for about 18 years. Ostriches, for about 50. A queen ant can live for 13 years. A tortoise can live to be about 150 years old, which is considerably older than even the oldest human beings.

Cats and Dogs:
Basic Stuff about Kitty and Pup

Reading a Dog's Body Language

- A dog who bows down to you with her front paws while keeping her rear end high is inviting you to play. Dogs do this to each other before a round of wrestling.

- A dog who rolls over on his back at your feet is showing you that you're the boss.

- A dog who licks your face is showing you affection. Puppies sometimes lick the mother dog's face to get food, so if your dog does this, she may be asking you for something.

- A dog who wags her tail at you may be happy to see you, or she may be nervous about you. A fast and squiggly wag usually means the dog is happy.

- A dog who holds his tail down low against his back legs is either sorry for having done something bad, or frightened about getting hurt or punished.

- A dog who lies on the ground asleep and twitches her nose, tail, and paws is probably having a great dream about chasing another animal.

- A dog whose ears and tail are pointing up is possibly frightened or angry. If his lips are pulled back, too, he may be thinking of biting.

Reading a Cat's Body Language

- A cat whose tail is twitching at the tip is probably mad about something.

- A cat with a curved tail is usually feeling curious about her surroundings.

- A cat whose tail is hanging low, and is fluffed out, is very possibly frightened.

- A cat who wags her tail doesn't mean the same thing as a dog who wags her's. A wagging tail on a cat often means the cat is in the middle of making a decision about something.

- A cat who arches her tail up high is probably about to get into a fight.

- A cat who rubs against you is putting her scent on you to mark you as one of her belongings.

The Hairball Question

Q: *Why do cats get hairballs, but dogs don't?*

A: Because cats clean themselves. The cat's tongue feels scratchier than a dog's tongue does. It feels a little like sandpaper. The cat uses her scratchy tongue as a kind of comb as she licks herself clean, and the tongue/comb pulls out a lot of fur. Naturally, the cat ends up swallowing some of the fur, and since cats can't digest fur, it forms into hairballs in the cat's body. Then the cat must cough the hairballs up, or poop them out.

Dogs, on the other hand, do not lick themselves clean, and don't have the scratchy kind of tongue. So when they shed, they just leave clumps of hair around the house.

The Fire Hydrant Question

Q: *What can a dog tell by sniffing a spot where another dog has peed?*

A: Humans don't know the answer to this question for certain, but some people are pretty sure that a dog can tell whether the last dog to pee in that spot was male or female, about how big the dog was, about how old the dog was, and even what kind of mood the dog was in.

Silly Dog and Cat Laws

- In Chicago, it's against the law to bring a French poodle with you to an opera house.

- In Duncan, Oklahoma, you can get arrested for insulting a dog catcher.

- In Sterling, Colorado, a pet cat isn't allowed outdoors unless it's got a tail-light.

- And in Cresskill, New Jersey, all cats are required to wear three bells, in order to scare away birds.

Cats don't have the tongue equipment to be able to taste sugar. So don't waste any candy on them.

Most dogs, unless they're hungry, are just as happy chewing on an ice cube as on a dog biscuit.

Cats, on average, live longer than dogs do — even though cats don't really have nine lives.

MindStumpers

Can you make one word out of D R E N O O W?

Answer: ONE WORD

Three fellas are hanging out on one side of a large lake. Some jerk on the other side of the lake aims a rifle at them, and shoots. One of the fellas sees the smoke from the rifle. Another hears the shot. And the third sees the bullet hit the water in front of him. Which of them first notices that the rifle was shot?

Answer: The speed of light is faster than the speed of sound, and the speed of sound is faster than a bullet. So the fella who saw the smoke knew first, the one who heard the shot knew second, and the one who watched the bullet hit the water knew last.

What four numbers between 2 and 12 can result only from one specific combination of two dice?

Answer: 2, 3, 11, and 12.

Out in Madison County there's a dark, one-lane 100-foot covered bridge. Yesterday morning Clint drove his pickup truck into one end of it as fast as he could and Meryl drove her car into the other end as fast as she could. Yet there was no crash. Why not?

Answer: They drove into the bridge at different times in the morning.

A woman kissed her husband good-bye, walked out their apartment door, locked it behind her, pressed the elevator button, and immediately realized that her husband had died. What happened?

Answer: Her husband was on a life-support system. When she pushed the elevator button, she realized the building's power had gone off.

Franklin Roosevelt thought up the name United Nations while in the shower.

Which animal has the longest gestation period (if this term stumps you, head for the nearest dictionary, after flushing): a) blue whale, b) African elephant, c) human being, d) salamander, or e) Dexter being.

Answer: The Alpine black salamander has the longest gestation period—sometimes a whole 38 months. While these salamanders can live at different elevations, the higher the elevation, the longer the gestation period. It's at about 4,600 feet that the gestation period gets up to 38 months.

Coconuts are seeds, not nuts.

Suppose there is an orchard of 172 apple trees, each averaging 332 branches, each branch with 41 leaves at the beginning of May. New leaves are added to each branch at the rate of 10 per week. How many leaves will be on the trees after 8 months?

Answer: None. Apple trees shed their leaves in the Fall.

What is the only thing you can put into a bucket that will make it lighter?

Answer: A hole.

A boat had a ladder on its side that swimmers used to get in and out of the water. Ten of the ladder rungs, each six inches apart, are visible above the water. If tide rises at at a foot per hour, how many of the rungs will be above the water after five hours of raising tide?.

Answer: Ten. As tide rises, so does the boat.

Brazil nuts are seeds, not nuts.

"WHADDAYA DOIN' IN THERE?"

It takes 200,000 frowns to make a permanent wrinkle.

The average drop of Heinz ketchup leaves the bottle traveling at 25 miles per *year*.

Porcupines each have more than 30,000 quills.

1,000,000,000 M&Ms are sold on any given day in America, and most of them are brown.

Your eyeballs are three and a half percent salt.

Your brain weighs only about three pounds, all but 10 ounces of it is water.

Cows give more milk when they listen to music.

Baby blue whales gain ten pounds every hour.

The saguaro cactus of the Arizona Desert grows less than one inch in its first 10 years.

Pigs and humans are the only animals that get sunburned.

To say just one word, you use over 70 muscles.

Animators drew nearly 6.5 million black spots for the film "101 Dalmatians."

Illinois Avenue, Go, B&O Railroad, Free Parking, and Tennessee Avenue are the five squares in Monopoly on which you're most likely to land.

Your brain uses less power than a 100-watt bulb.

On average, people spend more than five years of their lives dreaming.

Bats always turn left when exiting a cave.

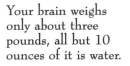

A restaurant in Mississippi called Hello, I'm . . . Jello serves over 400 dishes made from Jell-O.

Love It or Hate It
Great Words for Likes and Dislikes

Bathophobia means a serious dislike of baths.

Bibliomania means a great love for buying and collecting books.

Galeophilia means an extreme affection for cats.

Pedophobia means an abnormal fear of kids or dolls.

Teratism means a love of monsters.

Cynophobia means a major dislike of dogs.

Anthomania means an intense love for flowers.

Hippophile is a word for a person who adores horses (not hippos, strangely).

Mythomaniac is a word for a person who lies much too often.

Plutomania means an unnatural yearning to be rich.

Teratophobia means an abnormal fear of monsters.

Gymnophobia means an extreme fear of being naked. Makes sense, doesn't it?

Mel Blanc, the man who provided Bugs Bunny's voice, was allergic to carrots.

The first hankerchief was invented in 1743.

Knock, knock.
Who's there?
Bat.
Bat who?
Bat you can't wait to read
more of these jokes.

Knock, knock.
Who's there?
Tank.
Tank who?
You're welcome.

Knock, knock.
Who's there?
Catch.
Catch who?
Gesundheit.

Knock, knock.
Who's there?
Who.
Who, who?
Is there an echo in here?

Knock, knock.
Who's there?
Banana.
Banana who?

Knock, knock.
Who's there?
Banana.
Banana who?

Knock, knock.
Who's there.
Orange.
Orange who?
Orange you glad I
didn't say banana?

The number one rule of knock-knock jokes: The "k" is always silent.

Knock, knock.
Who's there?
Who.
Who, who?
Is there an owl in here?

Knock, knock.
Who's there?
Boo.
Boo who?
Don't cry, it's only a joke.

Knock, knock.
Who's there?
Ivan.
Ivan who?
Ivan awful headache since we started these really bad knock-knock jokes.

Knock, knock.
Who's there?
Hairy.
Hairy who?
Hairy up and finish these awful jokes.

And the Official Planet Dexter Knock-Knock Joke—

Knock, knock.
Who's there?
Dexter.
Dexter who?
Dexter halls with boughs of holly.

Saving Tillie
(Boo!)

Eric came home late one windy and almost moonless night, and found his mother standing at the screen door. She looked worried.

"Thank heavens you're home," she said. "Tillie has run off again."

Tillie was Eric's dog, an affectionate and playful Jack Russell terrier who loved to be near him. Eric often said that Tillie was worth 10 human friends put together, and he'd readily die to protect her from harm. As often as he could, he took Tillie everywhere. Sometimes, though, he couldn't. And on those occasions he tied her up in the yard. When she was a puppy, that worked fine. But four times within the past year, Tillie had chewed through the rope and run off looking for Eric.

Now she'd done it again.

"Any idea how long she's been gone?" Eric asked his mother, as he hurried back to his truck to begin searching for her. On such a dark night, Tillie could easily be hit by a car.

"I don't know when she left," his mother said. "But I'll bet she's gone off toward the cemetery."

That was one good thing about Tillie, thought Eric, as he buckled himself into the truck and took off down the dark road: Tillie was predictable. The first time she ran off, she came back on her own after a couple days, looking scraggly and frightened, but completely unharmed. That was about a year ago, and it scared him terribly. But the other times since then, Eric had been able to track her down as she trotted along the road that curved past the big oak tree and the cemetery. She always seemed to take that route. He wondered why.

As he approached that point in town, he scanned the road's edge. Sure enough, his headlights illuminated a little lump by the side of the road, off in the distance. Could it be Tillie? Was she moving? He squinted to try to see better.

But when he drove closer, he saw that it was a girl of about his age, kneeling over Tillie. He pulled up his truck behind them, and hurried to the girl's side.

"Tillie? Are you okay?" he said, barely acknowledging the girl.

"She's fine," said the girl, who was rubbing Tillie's stomach, to Tillie's obvious delight. "I just missed hitting her, but she's fine." It was then that Eric noticed the skid marks in the road, and the hissing sedan, its front end badly crumpled into the old oak tree. "I crunched up my car pretty good, but I'd rather die than hurt a little dog," said the girl, as Tillie licked Eric's face. "I take it she's yours?"

"Yes," said Eric, somewhat surprised to meet a girl who felt the way he did about dogs. "Are you from around here?"

The girl paused before answering. "I used to be," she finally said.

"I'm just visiting."

"Well," said Eric. "Can I give you a ride home? Your car looks totaled."

The girl said yes, and soon she and Tillie were in the front seat with Eric, as the girl directed him to her house. It was still nearly black out, so dark Eric couldn't quite see the girl. But he was increasingly interested in her. She was so good with Tillie, and she had risked her life to spare his dog. When she told him they were within a few blocks of her house, he got up his nerve.

"Listen," he said. "Would it be all right if I called you sometime?"

The girl laughed a little.

"Why are you laughing?" he asked, somewhat annoyed.

"Oh, it's nothing," said the girl. She dug around in her pocket until she found a receipt, wrote a number on the back of it, and handed it to him. "It's just that I know you'll only call me once. Here's my house, now. Bye." And she was off down the path to her front door.

The next day, Eric woke up and could think of nothing but the girl. He looked at the slip of paper she'd given him. "Julie," it read, and then her phone number. He decided to call her that night. The day passed very slowly, but finally he placed the call.

"May I please speak to Julie?" he asked the woman who answered the phone.

There was a silence, and then he heard the woman sob. "Who's calling?" asked the woman at last.

"It's Eric," he said. "I'm the one who met Julie on the road last night, and drove her home."

"That's not possible," said the woman. "Julie was my daughter, and she died a year ago last night exactly, when she crashed her car into the old oak tree as she was driving home, the dear girl, from getting my medication from the pharmacy. The police thought she must have been swerving to avoid an animal. Now, please. Don't call here again."

Shaken, Eric looked down at the piece of paper Julie had given him. He turned it over and saw that it was from Mertyn's Pharmacy, and it was dated a year ago last night.

Since 1886, the U.S. Patent Office has classified roller coasters as "scenic railways."

"WHADDAYA DOIN' IN THERE?"

Right or Wrong?

Sweat smells bad.

Wrong! Sweat has no odor. It's the bacteria that live and thrive in the sweat that smell bad. Soap and water get rid of the bacteria.

Fortune cookies are a traditional Chinese dessert.

Wrong! Fortune cookies were invented in America in around 1918 by a Chinese immigrant, George Jung.

George Washington had wooden teeth.

Wrong! George had the best teeth available in those days, ones crafted from walrus ivory.

Hollywood leads the world in movie making.

Wrong! India produces three times as many movies as Hollywood every year.

People who won't look you in the eye when they talk to you are untrustworthy.

Wrong! Psychologists have discovered that con artists and habitual liars are more likely to maintain steady eye contact than any other group of people.

The famous **"HOLLYWOOD"** sign was put up to promote the movie industry.

Wrong! It was put up in 1924 to promote a real estate development, "Hollywoodland." In 1945, when the sign was seriously deteriorating, the city of Hollywood took it over, fixed the first nine letters, and dumped the last four.

Chicago is called the "Windy City" because of the strong winds blowing in off of Lake Michigan.

Wrong! Chicago is not even among the country's top 20 windy cities. Chicago picked up the nickname because so many of its big-mouthed politicians are considered to be full of "hot air."

It is illegal to remove the tag on your mattress.

Wrong! Once you own it, you can do with the "DO NOT REMOVE" warning tag whatever you wish. That tag is for the retailer who sold it to you, not for you the consumer.

Bulls are outraged by the color red.

Wrong! Actually, bulls are color-blind. As far as they're concerned, you could be waving a nice blue plaid at them.

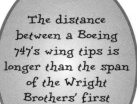

The distance between a Boeing 747's wing tips is longer than the span of the Wright Brothers' first flight.

Dear Planet Dexter

(Alien Ear Wax)

Dear Editors of Planet Dexter,

This kid sits next to me in math class. His ear wax looks different than mine. Do you think he's an alien? Should I let the school nurse know about this? The FBI?

Meanwhile, I'm looking forward to college.

Sincerely,

"Bored in math class"
(in Peabody, Massachusetts)

Dear Bored,

You actually see college in your future? As for the ear wax, it comes in two different varieties—wet and dry. The type of wax that you have is determined by your heritage. Most white, black, and Hispanic people have wet wax, which is oily, sticky, and tan colored. Most Asian and Native American people have dry wax, which is sticky, brittle, and gray.

Hope this helps.

Sincerely,
The Editors of Planet Dexter

Dear Planet Dexter
(Disappearing Money)

Dear Editors of Planet Dexter,

I'm stumped. I was told that Sal, Lee, and Eddie stopped at a hotel for the night and rented a room for $30. They each paid $10. That's a total of $30, right?

But oops!—the hotel clerk suddenly realized that the room was supposed to be only $25. So he gave a bellboy five $1 bills and asked him to return those to Sal, Lee, and Eddie. On the way up to their room, the bellboy realized that he didn't know how to divide the five $1 bills evenly among the three guests. So he cheated a bit. He told them that the room cost only $27, and gave each of them a $1 bill.

Then, guilt-ridden by his cheating, the bellboy ran over to his favorite charity and donated the other two $1 bills.

Here's where I get stumped. Sal, Lee, and Eddie each paid $9 for the room, right? That adds up to $27, right? And the bellboy gave $2 to the charity, right? That's a total of $29. What the heck happened to the other $1?

Sincerely,

"Stumped" (in Don Mills, Canada)

Dear Stumped,
We're on vacation this week.

Sincerely,
The Editors of Planet Dexter

Dolly Parton once lost a Dolly Parton look-alike contest.

Why?

Why do men have nipples?

So that when conversation around the family dinner table gets extremely boring, this question can be asked to liven things up. Seriously, males actually have the anatomical equipment in place to provide milk, but it lies dormant unless stimulated by estrogen, the female hormone. So maybe they're there in anticipation of some weird development that's not yet happened.

Why can't you feel the Earth turning?

Even though we're spinning at 1,000 miles per hour, it doesn't seem so because we're on the Earth, sharing its movement. It's like being on a jet airplane going along at about 600 miles per hour; being inside the plane, you aren't at all aware of the movement.

Why doesn't the United States own the moon, even though it got there first?

Because in 1967, the U.S. signed the Treaty on Exploration and Use of Outer Space, which established the lunar surface as the property of all mankind.

Why don't people eat turkey eggs?

Because they don't taste good and they feel weird (when a turkey egg is heated, it turns rubbery).

Why do we use only 10 percent of our brain?

That's a myth. We actually use nearly all of our brains in the course of a day, we just use different parts of it for different tasks.

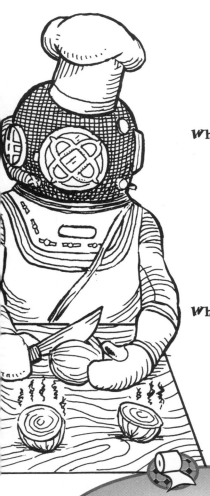

Why do people get goosebumps?

They're there to remind us that humans were once covered with hair which, when it got cold, stood on end to create a trap for air and provide a layer of insulation. Although all that hair is long gone, the skin still bristles, trying to get warm.

Why do people "cry" when they peel onions?

The eyes are very sensitive to the onion's volatile oils, which easily escape whenever an onion is sliced. When the oil in the air hits your eyes, your body snaps into a defensive position, producing tears to expel the irritant. Wearing a scuba diving mask would help a lot.

Why are flowers different colors?

We cannot tell a lie: we're not sure why flowers are different colors. However, some scientists suspect that together with a flower's smell, color attracts certain birds and insects. Different-colored flowers attract different insects and birds (hummingbirds go for red; bees can't even see red).

The word "aequeosalinocalcalinoceraceoaluminosocupreovitriolic" describes the composition of the spa waters at Bristol, in Gloucestershire, England.

The United States quit using gold coins in 1934, and ever since, getting your allowance is not nearly as much fun.

$

It costs 3 cents to make a dollar bill—and 7.8 cents to make a half-dollar coin.

$

If you're a billionaire, you can't afford to count your money. Really. *Think about it.* One billion equals a thousand millions (1,000,000,000). Let's suppose you could count at a rate of 200 per minute (that's not a bad estimate because if you count once every second, you'll count to 60 in a minute). So you could count to 12,000 in an hour or 288,000 in a day. Counting 365 days a year would take you 9,152 years, 34 days, 5 hours, and 20 minutes to count to a billion. Phew! You'd be outta here long before you could spend it.

$

Total allowances for American kids add up to $8.6 million! **WOW!**

Americans spend over $400 million on *toys* every day.

TEACHER: If you found 1 quarter, 2 dimes, and a nickel in one pocket and a $20 bill in the other pocket, what would you have?

STUDENT: Somebody else's pants.

$

The *nickel* is actually made of a mixture of copper and nickel; the penny is made of copper-coated zinc alloy.

United States currency *paper* is fluorescent under ultraviolet light.

The *ink* is slightly magnetic—not enough for refrigerator magnets to detect, but enough for special machines to notice.

Dimes, quarters, half-dollars, and dollars have a *copper* core covered with alloy of copper and nickel.

$

The average coin circulates for 15 to 20 years. (Think about how many people might have touched it and where it's been. Maybe your great-great-grandfather who you never met once had it! Maybe Bill Clinton used it for a coin trick. Maybe it was in your own hands five years ago—and now it's back!)

$

The average life span of a $1 bill is

a. 48 hours

b. 49,467 hours

c. one week

d. one full moon

e. about the length of summer vacation

f. 17 to 18 months

g. 13 years

Answer: **f.**

$

Do you bring your wallet along when go to the toilet? If yes, and you've got a bill (no!—not a "bill" like "Bill Clinton," but a "bill" like a one-dollar or twenty-dollar "bill"), rub its surface with some toilet paper. Look at the toilet paper. **See that?**

"Money in Oz! Did you suppose we are so vulgar as to use money here? If we used money to buy things, instead of love and kindness and the desire to please one another, then we should be not better than the rest of the world."

—The Tin Woodsman

The United States Treasury claims that what you see is ink. Your federal government further claims that this little experiment is proof that the Treasury uses a secret formula to create a special ink that never completely dries! But to us Editors of Planet Dexter, it just looks like dirt. Look at the tissue again. *What do you think?*

9

All products of 9 have digits that, when added together, equal 9. Really.

Like 9 x 6 = 54 and 5 + 4 = 9

Or 3 x 9 = 27 and 2 + 7 = 9

Or even really big-time multiplication problems like

9 x 201 = 1,809 and

1 + 8 + 0 + 9 = 27 and

2 + 7 = 9

Weird. Especially*Weird.*

37

Think of any three-digit number in which all digits are the same. For example, 333. Add the digits (3 + 3 + 3 = 9).

Divide the original number by the sum of its digits (333 ÷ 9 = 37). There's that weird number: 37.

Let's try some others.

111 ÷ 3 = 37

222 ÷ 6 = 37

999 ÷ 27 = 37

Weird. Especially*Weird.*

A 10-gallon hat holds about a gallon.

7

The next time you're scheduled to sit here, on the pot, bring along a calculator and do the following problems.

1 ÷ 7 = _____

2 ÷ 7 = _____

3 ÷ 7 = _____

4 ÷ 7 = _____

5 ÷ 7 = _____

6 ÷ 7 = _____

Get a load of that! In each answer, there is a sequence of numbers that endlessly repeats itself. See it? Right! It's 142,857. No other number does that.

Weird. Especially Weird.

9 again

Do you still have that calculator you sneaked into the bathroom for the weird number 7? Good. Try this.

Divide 1 by 9 (1 ÷ 9).

Now try 2 ÷ 9.

and then 3 ÷ 9, and so on and so on.

Weird. Especially Weird.

11 and 9091

Back to the calculator. Think of any five-digit number that does *not* begin with 0 . . . like 15658 or 22222 or 31772, and multiply it by 11.

Now multiply that answer by 9091. And **holy smokers!** Look at that answer! It's that original five-digit number—twice!

(Warning: Because some calculators don't have enough slots for ten digits, you may need a pretty fancy calculator for this weird thing to work perfectly.)

Brain Teasers

What word is it that when you take away the whole, you have some left?

Answer: Wholesome.

Start spelling each word as you count, starting with one. High how do you have to count before you use the letter "a"?

Answer: One thousand (remember that 101 should be spelled "one hundred one," not "one hundred and one"— that would be like writing 84 as "eighty and four").

What five-letter word does every Harvard graduate pronounce wrong?

Answer: The word "wrong."

Write the number *one hundred* using six 9's.

Answer: 99 + 99/99.

How can you cut a wheel of cheese into eight equal portions with just three straight cuts of a knife?

Answer: Cut the wheel into quarters (that'll take two cuts), stack the quarters on top of one another, and cut that stack in half.

America's favorite colors: Number one, blue. Then red, green, white, pink, purple, and orange.

What walks on four legs in the morning, two legs during the day, and three legs in the evening?

Answer: A human: on four as a baby, then on two legs, then with a cane in the later years.

If it takes four women five days to dig six holes, how long will it take one man to dig half a hole?

Answer: There's no such thing as "half a hole." A hole is a hole.

Which one of the following would see best in total darkness: an owl, you, or a bat?

Answer: None. Nothing can see in total darkness.

If you looked in the mirror and saw your image holding the letter "b" in your right hand, what would you actually be doing?

Answer: Two things: 1) holding the letter "d" in your left hand; and 2) wasting valuable time in the bathroom when you should be reading this book.

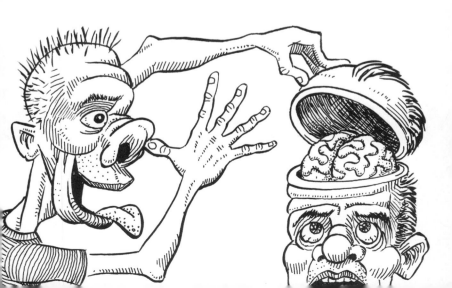

BallMania

A kooky Australian experiment in which a giant Superball was dropped off a skyscraper was a real bomb. The huge ball cracked on impact, sending jagged pieces bounding down the street and through shop and office windows.

In 1984, some guy named Albert Lucas juggled 10 balls simultaneously.

Every December near Katmandu, Nepal, a three-day polo contest is held in which elephants—not horses—are ridden by the players. The colorful elephants, with their faces and sides brightly painted, seem to understand the game, following the ball up and down the field, constantly moving into the best position for the player to swing his or her mallet, and never picking up the ball with their trunks as they could easily do. For several years the games were played with a large soccer ball, but the elephants took such delight in squashing the soccer balls that the players went back to regulation wooden polo balls.

Between 1950 and 1978, Francis A. Johnson built a string ball 12 feet, 9 inches in diameter, 40 feet in circumference, and weighing 11 tons.

Today's bowling comes from the ancient German game of Heidenwerfen (Hi-Den-Were-Fen), which means "knock down pagans."

On February 5, 1974, Mats Wermelin, age 13, scored all 272 points in a 272–0 win at a regional basketball tournament in Stockholm, Sweden.

Four hundred years ago in Mexico, the Aztecs played "Ollamalitzli," a game that closely resembled basketball. Now get a load of this: if the solid rubber ball was put through a fixed stone ring, the player who did so was entitled to the clothing of all the spectators.

In 1962, Australian meteorologist Nils Lied hit the longest golf driver ever: 2,640 yards, about 1-1/2 miles (across ice in Antarctica).

In golf you're penalized two strokes if you lose your ball. So why aren't you rewarded two strokes if you find somebody else's lost ball?

With the help of a $50,000 catapult now under development, the International Hurling Society ("Dedicated to the art, science, and history of throwing things") of Forth Worth, Texas, is planning to hurl a Buick 250 yards (that the length of two and a half football fields). The group has already tested smaller catapults, including a 25-foot model that can fling a toilet. Dr. John Quincy, a dentist and spokesperson for the International Hurling Society, notes, "The sight of a toilet flying almost 200 yards through the air is one of the magnificent things I've ever seen."

Yo! Spherical Rap ...

Before you try to rap on balls
You would be wise
To use your eyes
To memorize
This list of words
That rhyme with ball
So you won't get stuck
Like we just did.

Aerosol All Awl Alcohol Atoll Appall Bawl Befall Brawl Call Catcall Catchall Caterwaul Carryall Cholesterol Clairol Coverall Crawl Disenthrall DeGaulle Doll Drawl Enthrall Fall Folderol Forestall Freefall Firewall Gall Geritol Hall Haul Install Landfall Loll Lysol Miscall Moll Maul Montreal Nepal Nightfall Overhaul Overall Pall Paul Pitfall Parasol Pratfall Protocol Rainfall Recall Seawall Snowfall Stonewall Stall Shawl Scrawl Senegal Sprawl Small Squall Tall Trawl Tylenol Wall Waterfall Windfall Wherewithal Whitewall Warhol Yal Y'all

Ball, Louisiana, is apparently the only town in American named simply "Ball." It is considered to be a well-rounded place.

"All I had to do was keep turning left."
—George Robson, after winning the Indianapolis 500

"If they were faked, you would see me in more of them."
—Rod Gilbert, New York Rangers right wing, on being asked if hockey fights are faked

"You drive the car, you don't carry it."
—Janet Guthrie, race-car driver, downplaying the importance of strength in her sport

"If I was going to get beat up, I wanted it to be indoors where it was warm."
—Tom Heinsohn, Boston Celtics forward, on why he turned down a football scholarship

"We were so poor, every Christmas Eve my old man would go outside and shoot his gun, then come in and tell us kids that Santa Claus had committed suicide."
—Jake Lamotta, professional boxer

Humans are the only animal that sleep on their backs.

"All I can tell 'em is I pick a good one and sock it. I get back to the dugout and they ask me what it was I hit and I tell 'em I don't know except it looked good."
—Babe Ruth

"Sports is the toy department of human life."
—Howard Cosell

"You don't really see a muscle as a part of you. You see it as a thing. You look at it and it doesn't even seem to belong to you. You form it. Just like a sculpture.
—Arnold Schwarzenegger

"Jogging is very beneficial. It's good for your legs and your feet. It's also very good for the ground. It makes it feel needed."
—Snoopy

"It's just a job. Grass grows, birds fly, waves pound the sand. I beat people up."
—Muhammad Ali

"I went to a fight the other night, and a hockey game broke out."
—Rodney Dangerfield

Memorize This Stuff

(Impress Your Friends)

The Seven Wonders of the Ancient World

1 The Great Pyramids of Egypt (one is still the largest stone building in the world)

2 The Lighthouse of Alexandria (a big lighthouse before there were electric lights)

3 The Statue of Zeus at Olympia (40 feet tall and made of gold and ivory)

4 The Hanging Gardens of Babylon (very fancy terraced gardens)

5 The Temple of Artemis at Ephesus (marble temple with 127 columns)

6 The Colossus of Rhodes (110-foot-tall bronze statue of the Sun god, Helios)

7 The Mausoleum of Halicarnassus (gigantic marble tomb)

The Nine Planets in the Solar System

1 Mercury (moves around the Sun faster than any other planet)

2 Venus (hot planet with deadly acid clouds)

3 Earth (home sweet home)

4 Mars (red planet with a humongous canyon)

5 Jupiter (biggest planet)

6 Saturn (the one with the rings)

7 Uranus (planet with the longest seasons)

8 Pluto (small, cold, and dark)

9 Neptune (planet with fast winds)

America's favorite names for girl cats in order of preference are: Samantha, Fluffy, Misty, and Muffin.

PLANET DEXTER

Dear Planet Dexter
(Deadly Neighbors)

Dear Editors of Planet Dexter,

I'm desperate. I heard some kids in the garage next door talking. I thought they were just playing cards but now I'm not sure. Here's what I heard:

"Dudley, the dealer, shuffled the cards. Lefty cut the deck. Lulu, with her hat down low over her eyes, drew the wild card—a high spotter, lots of pips on it. Dudley reshuffled and dealt.

"Lulu's hand was lame; she fanned her cards and saw two deuces, a few pips, not a face card or ace in the bunch. She discarded the lows, drew from stock, chomped down on her Blow-Pop, and scowled.

"Lefty's hand was great—lots of aces and face cards, a couple of pairs, and a few highs. Life was sweet.

"Dudley fanned his cards, sorted them, popped his eyes, clutched his chest, and slid to the floor."

What happened? What were they talking about? Should I call the cops? Move out of the neighborhood? Help!

Sincerely,

"Desperate" (from San Diego)

Dear Stumped,

Don't worry. All's OK. Using this handy Dextionary, can you now figure out what happened?

ace	1) Some cool kid, usually one per neighborhood. 2) Any one of the four "A" cards in a deck of cards.
cut the deck	1) A far better situation than cut the cheese. 2) Split a deck of cards in half; then place the bottom half on top of the top half.
deck	A standard pack of 52 playing cards. If your deck has fewer than 52 cards, then, just like some of your classmates, you're "not playing with a full deck."

continued on next page

dead man's hand   A pair of aces and a pair of 8s, the very cards Wild Bill Hickok was holding in 1876 when he was shot during a card game at the Nuttal and Mann Saloon in Deadwood, South Dakota.

deuce
1) What a kid would be named if ever a kid was twice as cool as Ace.
2) A card with the number 2 on it.

discard
1) How some people who don't speak very well refer to a specific playing card, like they might say "Dis card beats dat card."
2) To put down a card you don't want at the end of your turn.

draw
1) What, in 1876, Wild Bill Hickok should have done much quicker.
2) To take the top card from the rest of the deck after the cards have been dealt.

face cards   The Jacks, Queens, and Kings of any suit. Face cards are also called "picture cards" or "high cards."

face down
1) Standard position for one who has just stepped in something gross.
2) When a card is on the playing surface and you can NOT see its picture or number side.

face up
1) Ironically, the thing you do when someone yells "DUCK!"
2) The position of a card when you can see the picture or numbers side of a playing card.

face value   Think of a card's face value as that card's number of points (you count points in most card games—it's usually how you keep score). The number cards have the same value as the number on them. For example, a 3 has a face value of 3 and a 10 a face value of 10 (a total of 13 points!).

fanning   Spreading out the cards in your hand, so just the corners of each card show.

hand
1) That thing with all the fingers at the end of your arm.
2) The cards you're holding in that thing with all the fingers at the end of your arm.

high   A card with a greater face value than some other card(s) it's being compared to; 4 is higher than 2 . . . 10 is higher than 4.

So, "Desperate," we hope this helps. Can you figure out what really happened to Dudley?

Sincerely,
The Editors of Planet Dexter

low — A card with a lower face value than some other card(s) it's being compared to; 3 is lower than 5 . . . 7 is lower than 9.

number cards — Any cards starting with the ace (Number 1) and numbered from 2 up to 10. Number cards are also called "spot cards."

pair — Any two cards that match by number or picture, like two 3s or two Jacks.

pip —
1) The heart, spade, diamond, or club symbol on a card that tells you what suit it is (see "suits"); also known as a "spot."
2) Only one Gladys Knight back-up singer.

shuffling —
1) A manner of walking really slowly in which the feet are not raised—most often used to get someplace you don't really want to go to.
2) Mixing the pack of cards before dealing.

spot — The symbol on a card that tells you what suit it is (see "suits"); also known as a "pip."

spot card —
1) Term used when you see some kid named Card, as in "I spot Card."
2) Any card with a number on it or an ace (as opposed to a "face card" or a "joker" or a "report card").

spot value —
1) The value, in dollars, of one dog named Spot;
2) Also see "face value."

stock —
1) What you have in reserve. If you buy nine frozen pizzas and eat one, you now have a stock of eight pizzas.
2) The cards that are left over after dealing.

suits —
1) A stifling, uncomfortable clothing concept most often used by annoying authority figures.
2) The four divisions in a deck of cards. Each suit contains 13 cards.

wild card —
1) A reckless and crazed card, one that runs around, curses, and throws food.
2) A card that can be used as whatever number or suit you want it to be.

Answer: Dudley had dealt himself the "dead man's hand."

Killer in the Back Seat
(Boo!)

Last year, outside Burlington, Vermont, a young veterinarian was driving home from her office one night when she noticed that she was running low on gas. She was annoyed that she hadn't thought to get gas earlier, as it was now dark and very cold outside. The empty country road she had taken was a short cut that brought her by only one lonely and quiet gas station. The guy in the gas station was creepy and there never seemed to be any other customers around. "Oh well," thought the veterinarian, "I guess this is what I get for being disorganized."

She spotted the gas station's lone, yellow light in the distance and took a deep breath. "Now don't get scared," she warned herself. "Plenty of people must get gas here, or else why would it still be in business?"

She put on her blinker to pull in, and her eyes darted from the hulking shapes of old cars to the machinery parts that were collected in heaps around the station. As she pulled up to the pump, the attendant came out of his office, pushing his greasy hair out of his eyes. The veterinarian rolled down her window and asked him to fill it up. She handed him her credit card and started to roll her window back up.

Abruptly, the attendant stuck his hand on top of the moving window and quickly rasped, "I'd appreciate it if you'd come in while I call to get the card approved. We don't get many cards around here, so they always ask a lot of questions. I think it would be quicker than me running in and out."

The veterinarian hesitated. She was scared to leave her safe, warm car, and she didn't like the idea of being in a small office with

the attendant. "I'm sorry, but I'm not dressed for the cold. I'll have to just wait here," she said. She started to roll up her window again, but the attendant wouldn't move his hand. He spoke again, his voice rusty with disuse. "Miss, I really think it'd be better if you came in. The card people always want all kinds of proof that the card isn't stolen, and it's just much easier if you're there with me."

Against all better judgment, the vet decided she would go in with him. There was something in the attendant's manner that was urgent, but now that she had heard him speak more than two words, she realized he probably wasn't as scary as he seemed. Just lonely and a little weird.

She opened the car door and followed him across the open area to the office. He opened the door and once they were both in, he slammed the door and locked it. The vet started to scream, but the attendant covered her mouth roughly and said: "Don't scream, miss. I'm sorry I had to drag you in here, but there's a man in the back seat of your car, and he has a knife. We need to call the police." Just then, the rear door of the vet's car was flung open, and a man dressed all in black went running out of the car and off into the dark countryside.

The vet and the attendant stayed in the office and when the police finally arrived, they found an 8-inch hunting knife on the floor behind the driver's seat. The man in black was never found.

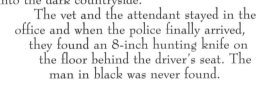

The oldest standing roller coaster in the world, Leap-the-Dips at Lakemont Park in Altoona, Pennsylvania, was built in 1902.

A **Big** Money Idea

Here's an **idea.** Maybe you can send a Planet Dexter message to people like Tom Cruise, the President of the United States, Michael Jordan, and your cousin. **Really! Maybe!**

Hold a $1 bill in your hand. Think about who else may have used that exact same $1 bill. Maybe your **cousin** used it to buy a soda at a store in the Boston airport.

Then *Tom Cruise* bought a newspaper at that same store with a $5 bill and got your cousin's $1 bill back in change. Then Tom Cruise flew to Seattle and spent your cousin's $1 bill on some **bubble gum** at the Seattle airport.

Then some **Secret Service** agent got your cousin's/Tom Cruise's $1 bill as change just before he hopped on an airplane with the **President** of the United States. Then that Secret Service agent lost your cousin's/Tom Cruise's $1 bill to the President in a poker game they were playing as they flew over Denver.

Then the President used your cousin's/Tom Cruise's/Secret Service agent's $1 bill to buy a birthday card for his wife. Then **Michael Jordan** came by that same store to buy a card for his best buddy and in change got your cousin's/Tom Cruise's/the President's $1 bill.

Which Michael Jordan spent at a grocery store where your grandmother shops, and **holy smokes!**—your grandmother took your cousin's/Tom Cruise's/the President's/Michael Jordan's $1 bill, added $4 more and mailed off all $5 dollars to you as a gift.

Weird, right?
Sorta awesome.

The United States bought Alaska from the Soviet Union for about 2 cents an acre.

HOW?

HOW do birds know if there's a worm in the ground?

Answer: A bird has very sensitive feet, which can feel the dirt vibrating as a worm crawls through it.

HOW is the following possible? The day before yesterday, Chris was 7 years old; next year she'll be 10 years old.

Answer: Today is January 1. Yesterday, December 31, was her 8th birthday (so the day before, December 30, she was 7). This year she'll turn 9, and next year she'll turn 10.

HOW many times can you subtract the number 5 from 25?

Answer: Once. After that you'll be subtracting 5 from 20.

HOW far can birds fly?

Answer: The bird that flies the farthest is the Arctic tern. It spends half the year in the Arctic and half in the Antarctic. A tern was once found in Australia that had flown over 14,000 miles—that's half-way around the world!—from where it was last spotted.

HOW many three-cent stamps are in a dozen?

Answer: A dozen (although most folks, at first, will say "four").

HOW did the boy do it? A hollow pipe, two-thirds filled with water, is cemented into the ground. Floating in the water is a ping pong ball. The mouth of the pipe is just slightly larger than the ping pong ball. Next to the pipe is a yardstick, a paper clip, and a magnet. For hours, two men have been attempting, without success, to get the ping pong ball out of the pipe without damaging the ball. Finally a boy walks over and within seconds, the ball is out of the pipe.

Answer: He peed into the pipe and the ball floated up and out.

HOW do fish sleep? With their eyes closed?

Answer: All fish sleep, although they never close their eyes. They can't: they have no eyelids! A fish's brain shuts out light and allows it to sleep, just the way your ears are open when you sleep, but your brain filters out what you need not hear.

> Duff is the decaying organic matter found on a forest floor.

HOW can somebody throw a golf ball a short distance, have it come to a complete stop, and then reverse itself?

The ball would not touch any other object and nothing would be tied to the ball.

Answer: Just throw the golf ball up in the air. It'll go a short distance, it will come to a complete stop, and then reverse direction.

HOW does the sun darken people's skin?

Answer: The color of a person's skin is caused by a substance called melanin, which protects you from harmful ultraviolet rays. How much melanin you have depends on your parents (if they've got a lot, too, you probably do, too). When you're in the sun, your body produces extra melanin and violá, you get darker.

HOW many times does the letter F appear in the statement below?

FREDDY FLIPPER WAS OF THE IMPRESSION THAT SUCCESSFULLY BEGGING OF HIS MOTHER FOR MORE SHOES OF THAT SORT WAS ESSENTIAL FOR KIDS OF HIS AGE.

Answer: Nine. Many readers miss the Fs in "OF."

HOW do pencil erasers work?

Answer: When you rub anything together, tiny pieces from one surface swap places with tiny pieces from the other surface. Erasers are made of rubber or plastic, and pencil marks are made of graphite. The graphite is picked up by the eraser and the eraser normally crumbles away as you rub. Those crumbles are the stuff you end up wiping or blowing away.

HOW is it possible that The Editors of Planet Dexter have a vacation house that is placed so that all four of its sides face south?

Answer: It's on the North Pole.

HOW many quarts of blood are in my body?

Answer: To find out, divide your weight by six.

WORDS

Each of the following represent a familiar term. For example, the first one depicts the word "editor-in-chief." Neat, eh? Good luck!

cheditorief

ONCE
4:30 P.M.

Hint: A classic beginning.

Answer: Once upon a time.

LOOKING
LOOKING **U** LOOKING
LOOKING

Hint: What you do a lot of if you're paranoid.

Answer: Looking around you.

DLIHC

Hint: I tried to help the kid, buddy up to him, but obviously, he's a . . .

Answer: Backward child.

RĚ-RĚ

Hint: My watch is running slow, I'll have to get it . . .

Answer: Repaired. RE-RE is a pair of REs.

---

casts
casts
casts
casts

Hint: A kind of crystal ball.

Answer: Forecasts (Four Casts).

S P A C E S

Hint: Texans love . . .

Answer: Wide-open spaces.

An Umbrella
SHEME

Hint: As for my girlfriend, if it's raining . . .

Answer: SHE meets ME under AN UMBRELLA.

ABCDEFGHI
JKMNOPQRS
TUVWXYZ

Hint: "We wish you a merry Christmas . . ."

Answer: Noel (no "L").

Edmond Rostand, French poet and playwright, hated to be interrupted while he was working, but he did not like to turn his friends away. Therefore, he took refuge in the bathtub and wrote there all day, creating such successes as *Cyrano de Bergerac*.

"WHADDAYA DOIN' IN THERE?"

Hair

- In general, all mammals (warm-blooded creatures who drink milk from their mothers when young) have hair of some kind or another, but sometimes it's hard to tell. A porcupine's hairs are its quills. A rhino's horn is made of many hairs fused together.

- Think all hair is either blond, brunette, red, white, or gray? Think again! A Kerry blue terrier is a type of dog that has a very dark blue gray kind of fur. And a Duroc pig grows hair that is naturally pink.

- Most of the world's population has dark brown hair.

- Some California surfers dye their hair surf-foam white using a mixture of peroxide (bleach) and Bisquick. Yup, a flapjack dye job. **Not recommended.**

- The darkest hairs on anyone's body are usually the eyelashes.

- Many dogs shed a lot of fur when the weather gets warmer. **Guess what:** the same is true of people. We shed more hair in the summer than we do in the winter, spring, or fall.

- Right now, about 90 percent of your hair is growing, about 10 percent of it has stopped growing and is just resting before *falling out*. Each hair rests for about 100 days before it falls out.

- The world record for long hair—at 13 feet, 10 1/2—is held by Mata Jagdamba, of India. If she wanted to, she could play jump rope with her own hair.

- If some nut offers you either a dollar for every hair on your head, or a dime for every hair that's not on your head, but on your body, which would you choose? **Go for the dimes!** There are about 100,000 hairs on your head but over five million on your body.

- Gold was discovered in Fairbanks, Alaska, on July 22, 1902. To celebrate that discovery, residents of the city get together every year in the third week of July and hold a beard and hairy-leg contest.

- The first toothbrushes were made from hog's hair. Gross, yes. But an appropriate tool for people who make pigs of themselves at dinner.

- At one time, in addition to cutting hair, barbers pulled teeth, performed surgery, and put leeches on people in order to bleed them. The red and white on the barber's pole stand for blood and bandages.

- The term "big wig," meaning an important person, comes from a time, in the 17th century, when you could tell what a person did for a living by the size of his wig. People in well-paying professions wore, yup, big wigs.

- The word "pogonotrophy" means "the growing of a beard," even though it sounds like an award you might get for pogosticking.

- A problem that's hard to solve is called a "hairy" problem. In computer programmers' slang, a problem that's really hard to solve is called "hair squared."

- There's a flower named Hairy Beardtongue. **Weird.**

The White House got its first toilet in 1825, when the president was John Quincy Adams (this gave us a new term for "toilet"—the "quincy.")

Presidential Quotations:
from Washington to Clinton

Note that many of these presidents lived before the American language came under the influence of the *political correctness* (PC) movement. So whenever one of these old guys with wigs who rode around on a horse and used an outhouse instead of a bathroom refers to "men" or to a "man," don't get upset; because what they probably meant was "person" or "people."

"Associate with men of good quality if you esteem your own reputation; for it is better to be alone than in bad company."
— George Washington, president from 1789 to 1797

"I must study politics and war that my sons may have liberty to study mathematics and philosophy."
— John Adams, president from 1797 to 1801

"Science is my passion, politics my duty."
— Thomas Jefferson, president from 1801 to 1809

"The diffusion of knowledge is the only guardian of true liberty."
— James Madison, president from 1809 to 1817

"Mrs. Monroe hath added a daughter to our society who, tho noisy, contributes greatly to its amusement."
— James Monroe, president from 1817 to 1825, in a letter to Thomas Jefferson regarding the birth of Monroe's daughter

"To furnish the means of acquiring knowledge is . . . the greatest benefit that can be conferred upon mankind. It prolongs life itself and enlarges the sphere of existence."
— John Quincy Adams, president from 1825 to 1829, on the establishment of the Smithsonian Institution

"One man with courage makes a majority."
— Andrew Jackson, president from 1829 to 1837

"Most men are not scolded out of their opinion."

—Martin Van Buren, president from 1837 to 1841

"I contend that the strongest of all governments is that which is most free."

—William Henry Harrison, president in 1841

"Here lies the body of my good horse, 'The General.' For twenty years he bore me around the circuit of my practice, and in all that time he never made a blunder. Would that his master could say the same!"

—John Tyler, president from 1841 to 1845, inscription on the grave of his horse

"No President who performs his duties faithfully and conscientiously can have any leisure."

—James Polk, president from 1845 to 1849

"Tell him to go to hell."

—Zachary Taylor, president from 1849 to 1850, reply to Mexican General Santa Anna's demand for surrender at the battle of Buena Vista

"An honorable defeat is better than a dishonorable victory."

—Millard Fillmore, president from 1850 to 1853

"The revenue of this country, levied almost insensibly to the taxpayer, goes on from year to year, increasing beyond either the interests or the prospective wants of the Government."

—Franklin Pierce, president from 1853 to 1857

"The ballot box is the surest arbiter of disputes among freemen."

—James Buchanan, president from 1857 to 1861

"If slavery is not wrong, nothing is wrong."

—Abraham Lincoln, president from 1861 to 1865

"Honest conviction is my courage; the Constitution my guide."

—Andrew Johnson, president from 1865 to 1869

"The right of revolution is an inherent one. When people are oppressed by their government, it is a natural right they enjoy to relieve themselves of the oppression, if they are strong enough, either by withdrawal from it, or by overthrowing it and substituting a government more acceptable."

—Ulysses S. Grant, president from 1869 to 1877

". . . the Constitution should be so amended as to lengthen the term of the President to six years, and so as to render him ineligible for a second term."
—Rutherford Hayes, president from 1877 to 1881

"All free governments are managed by the combined wisdom and folly of the people."
—James Garfield, president in 1881

"Men may die, but the fabrics of our free institutions remain unshaken."
—Chester Arthur, president from 1881 to 1885

"I am honest and sincere in my desire to do well, but the question is whether I know enough to accomplish what I desire."
—Grover Cleveland, president from 1885 to 1889 and 1893 to 1897

"Unlike many other people less happy, we give our devotion to a Government, to its Constitution, to its flag, and not to men."
—Benjamin Harrison, president from 1889 to 1893

"In the time of darkest defeat, victory may be nearest."
—William McKinley, president from 1897 to 1901

"Actions speak louder than words."
—Theodore Roosevelt, president from 1901 to 1909

"Nobody ever drops in for the evening."
—William Howard Taft, president from 1909 to 1913, on life at the White House

"I believe in democracy because it releases the energies of every human being."
—Woodrow Wilson, president from 1913 to 1921

"In the great fulfillment we must have a citizenship less concerned about what the government can do for it and more anxious about what it can do for the nation."
—Warren Harding, president from 1921 to 1923

"I've noticed that nothing I've never said has hurt me."
—Clavin Coolidge, president from 1923 to 1929

"Forgive your enemies, but never forget their names."
—John Fitzgerald Kennedy, president from 1961 to 1963

There are no photographs of Abraham Lincoln smiling (he probably never had a chance to read this book).
At six feet, two inches, and weighing as much as 326 pounds, William Howard Taft was not only the largest President of the United States, but the only one to get stuck in the White House bathtub.

"Whatever starts in California unfortunately has an inclination to spread."
—Jimmy Carter, president from 1977 to 1981

"The worst evil of disregard for some law is that it destroys respect for all law."
—Herbert Hoover, president from 1929 to 1933

"If you can't convince them, confuse them."
—Harry S. Truman, president from 1945 to 1953

"I hate war only as a soldier who has lived it can, only as one who has seen its brutality, it futility, its stupidity."
—Dwight Eisenhower, president from 1953 to 1961

"War is always the same. It is young men dying in the fullness of their promise. It is trying to kill a man that you do not even know well enough to hate. Therefore, to know war is to know that there is still madness in the world."
—Lyndon Baines Johnson, president from 1963 to 1969

"The ability to be cool, confident, and decisive in crisis is not an inherited characteristic but is the direct result of how well the individual has prepared himself for battle."
—Richard Nixon, president from 1969 to 1974

"A government big enough to give you everything you want is a government big enough to take from you everything you have."
—Gerald Ford, president from 1974 to 1977

"Excellence does not begin in Washington."
—Ronald Reagan, president from 1981 to 1989

"If anyone tells you that America's best days are behind her, they're looking the wrong way."
—George Bush, president from 1989 to 1993

"There is nothing wrong in America that can't be fixed with what is right in America."
—Bill Clinton, president from 1993 to present

"Be sincere; be brief; be seated."
—Franklin D. Roosevelt, president from 1933 to 1945, on speechmaking

Matches

1. Emma M. Nutt

2. The Bird of Prey

3. Jackie Coogan, child actor

4. Shirley Temple, child actor

5. Harp

6. Dexterbellyhugé

7. 22 inches in diameter

8. a 310-pound St. Bernard

9. 172 feet, 4 inches

10. 58 hours, 9 minutes

11. Pops Sanders

12. because he doesn't wear pants

a. The small metal hoop that supports a lampshade.

b. The world's first female telephone operator

c. Hugest dog ever

d. First person to catch a softball dropped off the Washington Monument

e. The Wright brothers' first plane

f. Millionaire by the age of six

g. The length of the longest unbroken apple peel

h. What happens on Planet Dexter when you eat too much

i. The size of the biggest gum bubble ever

j. Why Donald Duck comics were banned from libraries in Finland

k. Millionaire by the age of 10

l. The longest anybody's ever clapped

Tired of Mother's Day, Father's Day, and even Grandparent's Day? Check this out: The fourth Saturday of September is Kid's Day.

"WHADDAYA DOIN' IN THERE?"

STAR WARS FACTS

In July, 1973, George Lucas first approached Universal Studios to see if it might be interested in his idea for a film idea he called *Star Wars*. Universal turned him down (bad move).

Star Wars opened about two years later, on May 25, 1977, and within three months it had grossed $100 million, shattering all film revenues records up to that time. Within just six years, *Star Wars* tickets sales, worldwide, were over half-a-*billion* ($524 million).

Q: What was Harrison Ford working on when he was called in to read for the role of Han Solo?

A: Wood. He was working as a carpenter; his only part up to that time was the drag racer in Lucas's *American Graffiti*.

Q: What sources did Lucas repeatedly turn to as he wrote and developed the script for *Star Wars*?

A: Comic books and old serials such as *Buck Rogers*.

Q: Where did the idea for Chewbacca come from?

A: Lucas got the idea for Chewbacca one day as he watched his wife drive off with their Alaskan malamute, Indiana (who would later inspire the leading character's name in *Raiders of the Lost Ark*). Lucas liked the way the large shaggy mutt looked in the passenger seat. So he decided to create a character in the film that was a cross between Indiana, a bear, and a monkey.

Q: What's the name of the band that plays in the cantina that Obi Wan and Luke go to?

A: Schides Schondels.

Q: Upon the first screening of the film for executives of 20th Century Fox (who hated it—some sleeping through it, and others not "getting" it), what change was suggested for C-3PO?

A: That a moving mouth be added to the robot; otherwise, moviegoers could not possibly understood how he could talk.

Q: What vehicle do the Jawas drive?

A: A sandcrawler.

Q: On your videotape version of the film, why do Aunt Beru's lips often appear not to be moving with her speech?

A: Because her lines are all dubbed over. After the original theatrical release, Lucas felt that the real Beru's voice was too low, and needed to be changed.

Oops, a blooper. Right after the Death Star is destroyed, as Luke is descending the ladder out of his X-Wing and Leia comes running up to him, Luke mistakenly calls out her real name, yelling "Carrie!" (Princess Leia is played by the actress Carrie Fisher).

Neat. None of the spaceships ever moved during filming of the flight sequences. The motion was an optical illusion created by moving the cameras around motionless models.

Oops! Duck! Luke, Leia, Han, and Chewie are inside the Death Star's trash compactor. Suddenly it begins to compact. Luke yells into the comlink and the camera cuts to C-3POs comlink sitting on the table. Just then a security door opens, Stormtroopers march in, and Blam!—the actor playing the trooper behind and on the right of the lead trooper accidentally hits his head on the door frame.

A Distant Voice (Boo!)

Kevin's parents were going away for the evening, just to see some friends in the next town. Every other time they'd gone out, they'd hired him a babysitter, but this time they decided that he was finally old enough to take care of himself until they returned around midnight.

"Are you sure it'll be okay to leave him here?" asked Kevin's father. The family lived on a big farm, so there weren't any neighbors close by who could help Kevin if there were an emergency.

"I think so," replied Kevin's mother. "I know it still seems to us as though he's too young to be left alone, but he's got to start sometime."

They drove off, waving good-bye to Kevin. As if on cue, the skies began to darken. Obviously, a thunderstorm was brewing. But Kevin had never been frightened of thunderstorms, so neither he nor his parents worried.

Once his parents left, Kevin ate some macaroni and cheese his mom had left him, and then he went upstairs to his room to use his computer. He was so engrossed in surfing the Net that he didn't even really notice the storm until he heard a tremendous "CRACK!" The largest tree in the yard had been felled by lightning, pulling down the telephone wires as it thudded to the ground. Kevin's connection to the Internet was broken. He turned off the computer and stared out into the yard, where the fiercest storm he had ever seen was swirling and pounding.

It was then that he heard the phone ring. *How can the phone be working if the lines are down?* he wondered. But, thinking it was his parents calling, he answered it.

"There's a fire in your kitchen," said the voice on the other end of the line.

"What?" said Kevin. "Who is this? How do you know?"

"There's a fire in your kitchen," said the voice again. It had a southern accent, and sounded vaguely familiar to Kevin. Although he couldn't quite remember who the voice belonged to, he trusted it. He hung up the phone and went down to the kitchen.

Sure enough, a window in the kitchen had been smashed open by a falling branch, and lightning must have caught the curtains on fire, because they were blazing.

According to experts, "smart" kids watch the same TV same shows "average" kids do.

The phone rang again. Kevin picked up the kitchen extension and listened.

"There's a fire extinguisher under the sink," said the voice on the other end of the line, the same voice as before, with the same southern accent. "Take it out, read the directions on its side, and use it to put out the fire." Kevin had never seen a fire extinguisher in the kitchen. But he set down the phone's receiver, looked where the voice had told him to, found the extinguisher, pointed it at the curtains, and put out the fire.

Somewhat dazed now, he picked up the phone again, expecting to hear the voice. **But the line was dead.**

At that moment, his parents burst into the kitchen. They saw the broken glass and charred curtains and Kevin still holding the fire extinguisher.

"How did you know what to do?" they asked him.

"Someone called and told me," Kevin explained. But when his dad picked up the phone, the line was still dead. The whole family marveled at what a good thing it was that Kevin had put the fire out, as curtains burn very quickly and the fire could easily have spread to the rest of the kitchen and then the house.

The storm passed overnight, and the next day Kevin's father went out to inspect the downed power lines. He followed with particular care the phone line leading out of the house. One tree had pulled it down within sight of the house, but a second tree, a quarter-mile off, had snapped the phone line in two. When Kevin's father noticed where the broken end of the line lay, he gasped: its frayed end rested directly on the grave of Kevin's grandfather, a true southern gentleman who had passed away when Kevin was a toddler.

One-Minute Mysteries

If at noon Jack leaves Nashville for Tallahassee in a car traveling 15 miles per hour, and at midnight Jill leaves Tallahassee headed for Nashville in a car traveling 75 miles per hour, which car will be closer to Nashville when they meet?

Answer: Neither. They'll be at the same point when they "meet," and, actually, they'll be at the same distance from *anywhere*.

❓

If the day before the day after tomorrow will be Friday, and the day after the day before yesterday was Wednesday, what day is today?

Answer: Thursday.

❓

David and Barbara were found dead in a room that had an open window. On the floor were pieces of broken glass and a puddle of water. How did they die?

Answer: David and Barbara were goldfish. The wind knocked over their bowl on the window ledge.

❓

Police Officer Jim Campbell was walking down Lover's Alley, which runs behind several apartment buildings, when from behind the door of one building he heard screams, "Please, Jeff, don't! Please don't shoot me!" Then a shot rang out. Campbell ran through the door and into a laundry room where in the far corner, the dead body of the just-murdered woman was lying. Next to the body was the murder weapon, a silver-plated pistol.

Across the room, next to a row of washing machines, were three strangers. "I'm her lawyer," said one. "I'm her minister," said the second. "And I'm her driver," said the third.

"Over here, Reverend," Campbell said, "I'm arresting you on the charge of murder."

How did Officer Campbell know it was the minister?

Answer: Jeff is a man's name and the minister was a man. The lawyer and driver were women.

86

A woman walks into a bar and orders a glass of water. But instead of serving her, the bartender suddenly pulls out a gun and points it right at her face. After a couple of seconds, the bartender pulls the gun away, the woman thanks him, they shakes hands, and she leaves.

What just happened?

Answer: The woman had the hiccups and was hoping that the water would cure them. The bartender, being a nice guy, instead surprised her with the gun and successfully stopped the hiccups.

A father and his son were on a plane that crashed. The father was killed instantly and the son was rushed to a local hospital for immediate surgery. However, the surgeon looked at the patient and said, "I can't possibly operate on this boy, he's my son." How could that be?

Answer: The surgeon was the boy's mother.

A plane crashed directly on the border between the United States and Canada. In which country will the unidentified survivors be buried?

Answer: Neither, we hope. Survivors are not buried.

The ancient Egyptians had bowling alleys.

"Try another profession. *Any other.*"
—instructor of the John Murry Anderson Drama School, giving professional advice to would-be actress Lucille Ball, 1927

♦

"A genuine kiss generates so much heat it destroys germs."
—Dr. S. L. Katzoff, faculty member of the San Francisco Institute of Human Relations, 1940

♦

". . . leaves one with the feeling that the people it describes really do not matter; one is left at the end with nothing to digest."
—*The New York Times*, reviewing *The Sun Also Rises* by Ernest Hemingway

♦

"If your eyes are set wide apart you should be a vegetarian, because you inherit the digestive characteristics of bovine or equine ancestry."
—Dr. Linard Williams, British medical officer, 1932

♦

"Video won't be able to hold onto any market it captures after the first six months. People will soon get tired of staring at a plywood box every night."
—Darryl F. Zanuck, head of 20th Century Fox Studios, on television, 1946

"I don't like their sound. Groups of guitars are on the way out."
—Decca Recording Company executive, on turning down the Beatles, 1962

"The horse is there to stay, but the automobile is only a novelty—a fad."
—President of the Michigan Savings Bank, advising Henry Ford's lawyer not to invest in the Ford Motor Company, 1903

♦

"Man will never reach the moon regardless of all future scientific advances."
—Dr. Lee DeForest, inventor, 1957

In 60 seconds, your blood makes a complete trip through your body.

[to Burt Reynolds:] "You have no talent."

[To Clint Eastwood:] "You have a chip on your tooth, your Adam's apple sticks out too far, and you talk too slow."

—Universal Pictures executive, dismissing Burt Reynolds and Clint Eastwood at the same meeting, 1959

◆

"It is a vulgar and barbarous drama, which would not be tolerated by the vilest populace of France, or Italy . . . one would imagine this piece to be the work of a drunken savage."

—Voltaire, on *Hamlet* by William Shakespeare

◆

". . . on the whole too grim a picture to have wide appeal."

—*Kirkus Reviews*, reviewing *The Assistant* by Bernard Malamud

◆

"You ain't going nowhere . . . son. You ought to go back to drivin' a truck."

—Manager of the "Grand Ole Opry," firing Elvis Presley after just one performance

◆

"Heavier-than-air flying machines are impossible."

—Lord Kelvin, British mathematician, physicist, and president of the British Royal Society, 1895

"Your constitution [United States] is all sail and no anchor. . . . Either some Caesar or Napoleon will seize the reins of government with a strong hand; or your republic will be laid waste by barbarians in the twentieth century as the Roman Empire was in the fifth."

—Thomas Babington Macaulay, British Statesman, 1857

On April 11, 1994, *The Wall Street Journal* reported on legal efforts to define the term "butthead." The two leading candidates are 1) "a wise-cracking lout," and 2) "an endearing, fun-loving guy."

Checking Out Videos
(Watch Closely!)

In **Abbot and Costello Go to Mars**, they actually go to **Venus**.

In George Lucas's **Raiders of the Lost Ark**, when Indiana Jones enters the Well of Souls, *look at the wall carefully*; there are hieroglyphics of 3CPO and R2D2, the two robots from George Lucas's Star Wars.

In **Rambo III**, when Rambo steals a "Russian" helicopter, **check out** the American flag on the helicopter's rotor housing.

Stanley Kubrik (director of films such as **2001, A Space Odyssey**) always includes a **bathroom** scene in his movies.

In George Lucas's **American Graffiti**, take note of all the license plates to see if you can spot one that says "THX1138" (which *happens* to be the title of one of Lucas's earlier films).

Also keep your eyes on the license plate of the station wagon Richard Dreyfus and Teri Garr are driving in **Close Encounters of the Third Kind**. As they *smash* through several road blocks, the license plate keeps changing.

In one scene of **The Alamo**, (1960) you can see a stunt man falling into a **mattress**.

If you've got a friend who's not yet grasped the notion that movies are filmed out of sequence, have her watch the **Wizard of Oz** carefully. Dorothy's hair changes from mid-length to long to short as the movie progresses.

In **Camelot**, as King Arthur (Richard Harris) talks about how wonderful his medieval kingdom is, he's got a *Band-Aid* on his neck.

In **The Fortune Cookie**, Walter Matthau leaves one room and enters another **40 pounds** lighter! In the middle of this scene Matthau suffered a heart attack. By the time his hospital stay and recovery were completed and he returned to work, he had lost that much weight.

Apparently, Abraham Lincoln's ghost haunts the White House. Roosevelt once noted, "I was sitting in my study when one of the maids burst in on me in a state of great excitement. I looked up from my work and asked her what was the trouble. 'He's up there—sitting on the edge of the bed, taking off his shoes!' she exclaimed. 'Who's up where, taking off his shoes?' I asked. 'Mr. Lincoln!' the maid replied." Queen Wilhelmina of the Netherlands also saw the Lincoln ghost during a state visit in 1945. And there were several spottings during Jimmy Carter's administration.

Screen Quotes . . .

From the TV series *The Bob Newhart Show*—

Bob Hartley: *"Howard, what do you do when you're upset?"*
Howard Borden: *"Well, I've got a method—it always works. I go into a dark room, open up all the windows, take off all my clothes, and eat something cold. No, wait a minute, I do that when I'm overheated. When I have a problem I just go to pieces."*

It took 42 years for a letter mailed from an office in Eureka, California, to arrive at a different office in the same building. "Neither rain, nor snow . . ."

From the film, *The Wild One*—

Girl to Marlon Brando: *"Hey Johnny, what you rebelling against?"*
Brando: *"Whaddaya got?"*

From the TV series, *The Munsters*—

Herman Munster: *"You know, if Michelangelo had used me as a model, there's no telling how far he could have gone."*

From the film, *Fast Times at Ridgemont High*—

Sean Penn (Paraphrasing American history)*: "What Jefferson was saying was 'Hey! you know, we left this England place 'cause it was bogus, so if we don't get some cool rules ourselves— pronto— we'll just be bogus too.'"*

From the TV series, *The Dick Van Dyke Show*—

Buddy Sorrell: *"Wanna do something courageous? Come to my house and say to my mother-in-law, 'You're wrong, fatso!'"*

From the film, *Raising Arizona*—

Randall "Tex" Cobb: *"If you want to find an outlaw, you call an outlaw. If you want to find a Dunkin' Donuts, call a cop."*

From the TV series, *Cheers*—

Coach Ernie Pantusso (on banking): *"Why do they call them tellers? They never tell you anything. They just ask questions. And why do they call it interest? It's boring. And another thing—how come the Trust Department has all their pens chained to the table?"*

From the film, *North Dallas Forty*—

Nick Nolte (suggesting a slogan for Bo Svenson's restaurant): *"Jo Bob's Fine Foods—Eat Here or I'll Kill You."*

From the film, *I Was a Teenage Frankenstein*—

"I know you have a civil tongue in your head. I sewed it in there myself."

From the film, *The Wizard of Oz*—

Judy Garland: *"And oh, Auntie Em, there's no place like home."*

BugMania

Termites have micro creatures in their stomachs to help them digest wood. Because these little stomach creatures produce a lot of methane, termites fart like crazy.

A queen ant can lay 30,000 eggs a month for up to 10 years.

Butterflies have 12,000 eyes.

Fleas jump 130 times their own height. That's like a person jumping over a 65-story building.

Ants can live for 16 years.

Say this 10 times, fast: "Moths munch mushy mushrooms."

The tiny silver eggs that mother lice stick to the hairs on a lice-infected head are called "nits." Nits often have to be removed by picking through each strand of hair. Thus, the term "nit picky" for people who are very fussy.

Cockroach blood is white.

Mosquitoes flap their wings 1,000 times every second.

Bees are more likely to sting people on windy days than in any other kind of weather.

Queen bees can lay 3,000 eggs a day.

Hornets eat houseflies. Some American settlers used to hang hornets' nests in their homes to get rid of the flies.

The world's smallest spider is half the size of this period.

Dragonflies can fly 35 miles per hour—faster than any other insect.

People who study bugs are called "entomologists."

Mosquitoes are more likely to bite you right after you've eaten a banana.

Queen bees use their stingers only to kill other queen bees.

Queen termites can live for 100 years.

If ants were human sized, they could run five times as fast as a record-breaking Olympic runner.

Only female mosquitoes bite humans.

The killer bees' territory is growing by 300 miles per year.

Flies can carry germs 15 miles away from their source.

Queen bees can live for seven years.

Mosquitoes can get athlete's foot.

Love is the fart of every heart For when held in, doth pain the host.
—John Suckling, poet

Some people consider chocolate-covered ants a delicacy.

Some tarantulas can go for two years without eating.

Yellow and black markings on an insect or reptile can mean that this animal is dangerous.

If you put 40 fireflies in a jar, you should be able to read by the light they make.

Other Names for **Money**

(liven up your school reports!)

Ace

Beans

Berries

Bits

Bob

Boodle

Bread

Bucks

Cabbage

Cash

Chips

Deuce

Dinero

Do-Re-Mi

Dough

Burping while lying on your back is a lot harder than burping while you're sitting or standing.

Gelt

Greenbacks

Jack

Lettuce

Lolly

Long Green

Lucre

Mazuma

Moola

Oof

Palm Oil

Quid

The Read

Rhino

Sawbucks

Scratch

Shekels

Skins

Simoleons

Snaps

Spondulix

Spot

Vishneggies

Yard

First Flicks

Match the movie star with his/her first film (including role).

movie star

1. Tom Cruise

2. Madonna

3. Harrison Ford

4. Tom Selleck

5. Kevin Costner

6. Jeff Goldblum

first film (role)

a. *Dead Heat on a Merry-Go-Round* (bellhop)

b. *Death Wish* (thug punk)

c. *Endless Love* (teenage arsonist)

d. *Sizzle Beach, USA* (wealthy rancher)

e. *A Certain Sacrifice* (Bruna, a very minor character)

f. *Myra Breckinridge* (talent agent)

Answers: 1. c; 2. e; 3. a; 4. f; 5. d; 6. b.

"WHADDAYA DOIN' IN THERE?"

97

Really Bad Jokes

Why was the farmer so successful?
He was out standing in his field.

What did the astronaut see on the stove?
An unidentified frying object.

Did you hear about the fire at the circus?
The heat was in tents.

Where does a bird go when it loses its tail?
To the retail store.

What goes up when the rain comes down?
An umbrella.

What's black and white and read all over?
A newspaper.

What has four wheels and flies?
A garbage truck.

What did one torpedo say to the other torpedo?
Are you sinking what I'm sinking?

Answer the phone.
But it's not ringing.
Why wait until the last minute?

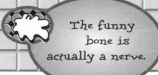

The funny bone is actually a nerve.

What goes mooz, mooz?
A plane flying backwards.

Why is the river so rich?
It has two banks.

A noise woke me up this morning.
What was it?
The crack of dawn.

Doctor, I've had a dime stuck in my ear for months.
Why didn't you come to me sooner?
I didn't need the money.

What does a pig write with?
A pig pen.

Doctor, I have carrots growing out of my ears. How did that happen?
I don't know. After all, I planted cucumbers.

Beth and her dog, Champ, went to a friend's house and started to watch a video tape that the friend had rented. About half way through the tape, Champ started to laugh, hysterically.
"Wow," said the friend, "I've never seen a dog laugh like that before. That's amazing."
"It sure is," said Beth. "Especially since he hated the book."

MegaWords

Klazomaniac
Someone who always feels like shouting.

Floccipaucinihilipilification
The action of estimating as worthless.

Misodoctakleidist
Someone who dislikes playing the piano.

Trichotillomania
A mental illness that causes people to want to pull out some of their own hair. A trichotillomaniac feels better once the hair is yanked out, and will sometimes pull out the hair of friends, family, or strangers.

Hebetate
To become stupid or boring.

Ablutomaniac
Someone obsessed with taking baths.

Trichophagia
The very harmful practice of eating a lot of hair .

Pneumonoultramicroscopic-silicovolcanoconiosis
a lung disease

Nuestra Senora Reina de los Angeles
The city of Los Angeles' full name.

Nash-gob
An arrogant gossip.

Palilalia
Helplessly repeating a phrase faster and faster.

Ranarium
A frog farm.

Vespertilonize
To turn into a bat.

Spitting watermelon seeds is almost as popular as eating watermelon. There are even watermelon-seed spitting contests. The world record for watermelon-seed spitting goes to Lee Wheelis of Texas, who spat a seed 68 feet, 9-1/4 inches. The next time you eat watermelon, see if you can break that record.

BIG (And Small) Deals

BIG DEAL: Robert Wadlow, born in 1918, grew to be 8 feet 11 1/2 inches tall. He was still growing at the age of 26, and probably would have reached 9 feet tall if he hadn't died young.

SMALL ONE: A two-year-old (fully grown) Yorkshire Terrier was once measured to be only two-and-a-half inches tall at its shoulders.

BIG DEAL: The largest known flower grows on the parasitic stinking corpse lily (quite a name!), found in Southeast Asia. It can grow to three feet across. And it can weigh 15 pounds.

SMALL ONE: The nest of certain hummingbirds are only about the size of a thimble.

BIG DEAL: Some bats grow wingspans of about six feet.

SMALL ONE: The smallest thermometer ever made measured about 1/50th the diameter of a single human hair.

BIG DEAL: The anaconda snake of South America, when fully adult, can weigh 500 pounds. An awful lot of snake.

SMALL ONE: The smallest newspaper ever printed was probably the Daily Banner of Roseberg, Oregon. It measured just three inches by three and three-quarters inches.

BURP!

The Lunch Box Pop Art Museum, located in Columbus, Georgia, displays more than 3,000 lunch boxes.

BIG DEAL: The African bush elephant stands over 10 feet tall (measured at the elephant's shoulder) and weighs over six tons.

SMALL ONE: The smallest spiders, called Patu marplesis, are so small that one could comfortably hide in the period at the end of this sentence.

BIG DEAL: The eyeball of the Atlantic giant squid can measure almost 16 inches in diameter. The better to see you with.

SMALL ONE: The smallest known frog grows to be less than half an inch long.

BIG DEAL: The seed of a double coconut tree can weigh 40 pounds.

SMALL ONE: The smallest bone in the human body is the stapes, or stirrup bone, in the ear. It measures about one-tenth of an inch long.

Only one in *two million* people are killed by being struck by lightning.

EYE, CAPTAIN!

How come?
Commonplace Mysteries

How come whenever someone lives in an apartment on television, that person always keeps his or her apartment door unlocked, and always has neighbors who feel completely welcome to walk right into the apartment at any time of the day or night without knocking?

How come, on diaper commercials, urine is always represented by blue liquid? Why blue?

How come people in cereal commercials almost always eat their cereal out of clear glass bowls, and how come the milk on that cereal and in the pictures of cereal on cereal boxes always looks as though it's really white paint, instead of milk?

How come when people drive on TV or in the movies, they always move the steering wheel back and forth so much? In real life, no one drives like that.

How come elevators break down so often on TV?

How come, whenever someone buys a bag of groceries on TV, there's always a loaf of french bread and a stalk of celery sticking out of the top of the bag?

How come, on a TV sitcom, you can see a person in a shower or in bed or wearing a bathing suit, but you never see anyone sitting on the toilet?

How come no man on TV knows how to iron a shirt? And how come whenever someone doesn't know how to iron something on TV, that person ends up burning an iron-shaped hole into the fabric?

How come so many people on TV get amnesia? How come whenever someone on TV has laryngitis, they can't make any noise with their voice at all, whereas in real life you can still be heard a little?

How come, on TV, a woman wearing thick red lipstick can kiss a man, and yet none of the lipstick comes off on the man's lips?

How come, on TV, whenever someone unwraps a gift, the top of the gift box is wrapped separately from the bottom of the gift box, so all the unwrapper has to do is untie the bow and lift off the top of the giftwrapped box (no ripping, no wadding up of the paper, no ugly shoe-boxes revealed beneath the paper)?

How come, on TV, people never sneeze unless they're coming down with a cold, and they never cough unless they're about to develop a serious illness?

How come whenever a man is supposed to meet a woman in a movie or a TV show, the two of them bump into each other in a hallway, and all of their stuff goes flying all over the place, and they stare into each other's eyes like love-struck puppies as they pick the stuff up?

The Odd Bod

A Little Quiz

1. Vomit is greenish because
   a. you've eaten your vegetables
   b. bile from your intestine makes it that color
   c. your tonsils stain it green on the way out

2. Your body produces a whole new layer of skin every
   a. two years
   b. seven and a half years
   c. 28 days

3. In the space of a minute, you blink
   a. 12 times
   b. 145 times
   c. 20 times

4. During a sneeze, air whooshes out your mouth at
   a. 40 miles an hour
   b. 10 miles an hour
   c. 2 miles an hour

5. Household dust is made up of
   a. mostly fibers from clothing
   b. mostly hairs that have fallen out of peoples' heads
   c. mostly dead skin cells

6. On a square inch of your leg skin
   a. 20 bacteria live
   b. 8,000 bacteria live
   c. no bacteria live, if you've taken a bath in the last week

7. Most people burp about
   a. once a week
   b. once a day
   c. 15 times a day

8. Projectile vomiting, in which a vomit stream shoots rapidly across large distances, is most common among
   a. people on a cruise
   b. young children
   c. women who are pregnant

9. If you see a piece of poop, you can safely guess that
   a. about half of the material in it is bacteria
   b. almost all of the material in it is bacteria
   c. only a tiny bit of the material in it is bacteria

10. The average person's large intestine is
   a. half a mile long
   b. six and a half inches long
   c. five feet long

11. An empty bladder looks like
   a. a small, firm, grape
   b. a peanut
   c. a shriveled prune

12. Spit is
   a. mostly water
   b. mostly mucus
   c. mostly liquid salt

Sign
LANGUAGE

The longest living gold-fish ever was Fred. He lived for 41 years.

The following comes from the National Association for the Deaf.

If you have questions about this alphabet or deafness, write to the National Association for the Deaf at:
814 Thayer Avenue, Silver Spring, Maryland 20910

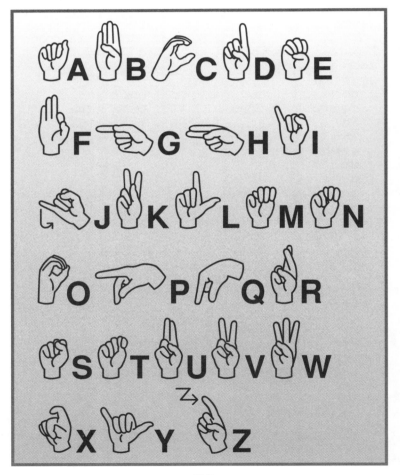

Superstitions Explained

Opening an Umbrella in the House is Bad Luck

This belief came about because, at one time, umbrellas weren't made very well. The spring in them that helped the umbrella expand was awkward, and if you opened an umbrella carelessly in the house, someone might get hurt.

"See a pin, pick it up. All day long you'll have good luck."

Ever heard that one? It probably grew out of the knowledge that if a pin is lying on the ground, someone might step on it and get hurt (bad luck). Shiny things, like pins, were once considered kind of magical, and the shedding of any small amount of blood was thought to be a sign of future disaster.

It's Bad Luck to Spill Salt

Ever seen someone throw a pinch of salt over his left shoulder after spilling it? That's because spilling salt has long been believed to be bad luck. Salt is associated with tears, and people once believed that if you spilled salt, you were destined to shed as many tears as would dissolve the spilled salt. Others believed that every grain of salt spilled stood for a tear that the spiller would cry in the near future.

Breaking a Mirror Means You'll Have Seven Years of Bad Luck

Mirrors were once very expensive, and difficult to replace. Rich families, concerned that their servants would break the mirrors, may have told their servants that breaking a mirror would cause seven years of back luck. Likewise, it might take a poor family seven years to earn enough money to replace the mirror if it were broken.

The most-watched film in history is *The Wizard of Oz.* Over one billion people have seen it.

Our Favorite Tongue Twisters

(The Perfect Place to Practice These? In the Bathroom!)

Rubber baby buggy bumpers.

The sixth sick sheik's sixth sheep's sick.

The skunk sat on a stump; the skunk thunk the stump stunk, but the stump thunk the skunk stunk.

How much wood would a woodchuck chuck, if a woodchuck would chuck wood? A woodchuck would chuck all the wood if a woodchuck could chuck wood.

Pull the pool pole, please.

Toy boat or troy boat. (Be sure to repeat at least six times.)

She sells seashells by the seashore.

The sinking steamer sunk.

Something to Think About

What if the distance between bases on a baseball field wasn't 90 feet. Just think about that. Ask yourself: "What if it was 20 feet? Or 120 feet?" Would the game still be popular? More popular?

Just think. Thinking is a good thing to do.

For example, about this baseball 90-feet thing: if the distance were instead 20 feet, wouldn't the field be smaller? Which means that an average stadium could fit more seats . . . that means more people . . . more people eating stadium stuff like hot dogs? It follows that 20 feet would be better for the hot dog industry and, in the end, Oscar Meyer would be richer than Oscar already is.

So you see, thinking is really a valuable thing to do.

Let's Face It

A *bibcock* is a faucet with a bent-down nozzle.

Match the bill (U.S. currency) with the face (that appears on it)

1. one
2. two
3. five
4. ten
5. twenty
6. fifty
7. hundred
8. five hundred
9. one thousand
10. five thousand
11. ten thousand
12. one hundred thousand
13. twenty billion

a. Ben Franklin
b. Ulysses S. Grant
c. Andrew Jackson
d. President Dexter
e. Abraham Lincoln
f. Thomas Jefferson
g. George Washington
h. Woodrow Wilson
i. Salmon P. Chase
j. Grover Cleveland
k. James Madison
l. William McKinley
m. Alexander Hamilton

Answer: 1. g; 2. f; 3. c; 4. m; 5. c; 6. b; 7. a; 8. l; 9. j; 10. k; 11. i; 12. h; 13. d

---

The **10** Most Commonly Used Words in Written English

1. The
2. Of
3. And
4. A
5. To
6. In
7. Is
8. You
9. That
10. It

Every state has at least one nickname, and many have three or four. We've noted our **favorites** below.

STATE	NICKNAME
Alabama	The Heart of Dixie
Alaska	Land of the Midnight Sun
Arizona	The Grand Canyon State
Arkansas	The Land of Opportunity
California	The Golden State
Colorado	The Centennial State
Connecticut	The Constitution State, The Nutmeg State
Delaware	The First State, The Diamond State
Florida	The Sunshine State
Georgia	The Peach State, **The Goober State**
Hawaii	The Aloha State
Idaho	The Hawkeye State
Illinois	Land of Lincoln, The Praire State
Indiana	The Hoosier State
Iowa	The Hawkeye State
Kansas	The Cyclone State, **The Squatter State**
Kentucky	The Bluegrass State
Louisiana	The Bayou State
Maine	The Pine Tree State
Maryland	The Free State
Massachusetts	The Bay State
Michigan	The Wolverine State, The Lake State
Minnesota	The North Star State, The Gopher State
Mississippi	The Magnolia State, **The Mud-cat State**
Missouri	The Show Me State

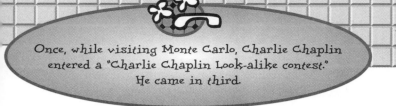

Once, while visiting Monte Carlo, Charlie Chaplin entered a "Charlie Chaplin Look-alike contest." He came in third.

Montana	Big Sky Country, **The Stub Toe State**
Nebraska	The Tree Planter's State, **The Bug-eating State**
Nevada	The Sage State
New Hampshire	The Granite State
New Jersey	The Garden State
New Mexico	The Cactus State
New York	The Empire State, Knickerbocker State
North Carolina	Old North State, **Tarheel State**
North Dakota	The Sioux State
Ohio	The Buckeye State
Oklahoma	The Sooner State
Oregon	The Beaver State
Pennsylvania	The Quaker State
Rhode Island	The Smallest State, The Ocean State
South Carolina	The Rice State
South Dakota	The Sunshine State
Tennesee	The Volunteer State, **The Hog and Hominy State**
Texas	The Lone Star State
Utah	The Beehive State
Vermont	The Green Mountain State
Virginia	Old Dominion
Washington	The Evergreen State
West Virginia	The Mountain State
Wisconsin	The Badger State
Wyoming	The Equality State, The Cowboy State

Riddles

Why is 6 afraid of 7?

Answer: Because 7 8 9.

What has a mouth but doesn't eat,
a bank with no money,
a bed but doesn't sleep,
and waves without hands?

Answer: A river.

If a person faints, what number should you bring him?

Answer: You should bring him 2.

As I was going to St. Ives,
I saw a man with seven wives;
The seven wives had seven sacks,
the seven sacks had seven cats,
the seven cats had seven rats.
Rats, cats, sacks, wives,
how many were going to St. Ives?

Answer: One (me).

What word begins with E, ends with E, and sounds as if it has only one letter in it?

Answer: Eye.

How can you make a witch scratch?

Answer: Take away her W.

If Washington went to Washington wearing white woollies while Washington's wife waited in Wilmington, how many W's are there in all?

Answer: There are no W's in "all."

What starts with T, ends with T, and is filled with T?

Answer: Teapot.

What does this describe?
Lives in winter,
Dies in summer,
And grows with its roots upward.

Answer: An icicle.

What does the following
rhyme describe?
Little Nanny Etticoat
In a white petticoat,
And a red nose;
The longer she stands
The shorter she grows.

Answer: A candle.

It wasn't my sister nor my
    brother,
But still was the child of
    my father and mother.
Who was it?

Answer: Myself.

What's this?
Thirty white horses upon a
    red hill,
Now they tramp, now they
    champ,
Now they stand still.

Answer: The teeth and gums.

How many jelly beans can
you put in an empty jelly-
bean jar?

Answer: Only one. After that
it's not empty.

What's the difference
between a counterfeit dollar
and a crazy rabbit?

Answer: One is bad money
and the other is a mad bunny.

What's this?
I come more softly than a
    bird,
And lovely as a flower;
I sometimes last from year
    to year
And sometimes but an
    hour.
I stop the swiftest railroad
    train
Or break the stoutest tree.
And yet I am afraid of fire
And children play with me.

Answer: Snow.

Paco and Millicent were stand-up comedians. They sometimes worked together and sometimes worked apart, but they both agreed that there was nothing they loved more than standing on the stage and making people laugh. For years and years they talked about their love of stand-up comedy, and by the time they were both old enough to retire, they had become wonderful friends.

One day during their retirement, they were sitting together at an oudoor cafe and talking about the good old days.

"What do you think, Paco?" Millicent asked. "You think maybe they have stand-up comedians in heaven?"

"Hmm," said Paco. He tried to picture a little stage in heaven where former stand-up comedians performed together. "Maybe so."

"Well, let's make a pact," said Millicent. "Whichever of us gets to heaven first will find a way to come back down to earth and tell the other person whether heaven's got stand-up comedians."

"Okay," said Paco, and they had a good laugh about the idea.

Five years passed, and Millicent died.

Paco almost forgot about their deal, but, now and then, he'd find himself listening to hear if Millicent was trying to tell him something from the great beyond.

One day, about six years after Millicent's death, Paco walked into that same cafe where they'd sat and talked about heaven. And there, sitting in the same chair where she'd sat before, was Millicent.

"Millicent!" he said. "I thought you'd never show! So tell me all about heaven! Do they have stand-up comedians there?"

"Well," said Millicent, "I have good news about that, and I have bad news."

"What's the good news?" asked Paco.

"The good news is that they've got the best stand-up comedians imaginable in heaven. You should see some of the stars I share the stage with now! The best of the best!"

"That's great!" said Paco. "And what's the bad news?"

"The bad news," said Millicent, "is that, tomorrow night, you're the opening act."

The 15 Longest
Rivers in the World

		length (miles)
1.	Nile, Africa	4,145
2.	Amazon, South America	4,000
3.	Mississippi-Missouri, U.S.	3,710
4.	Ob-Irtysh , former U.S.S.R.	3,460
5.	Yangtze, China	3,400
6.	Huang Ho, China	3,000
7.	Congo, Africa	2,718
8.	Amur, Asia	2,700
9.	Lena, former U.S.S.R.	2,680
10.	Mackenzie-Peace, Canada	2,635
11.	Mekong, Asia	2,600
11.	Niger, Africa	2,600
13.	Paraná, South America	2,530
14.	Murray-Darling, Australia	2,310
15.	Volga, former U.S.S.R.	2,290

The Handy Grave (Boo!)

Two bad boys with nothing better to do were hanging out near the town cemetery one October evening.

"I've heard," said the first bad boy, "that if you dance on a person's grave, you can feel the person in the grave knock on the inside top of his coffin to tell you to cut it out."

"No way!" said the second bad boy. "That's bogus. I'll go do it right now, if you want, and prove you wrong."

"Okay," said the first bad boy, and he went along to watch. Sure enough, the second bad boy selected a grave and started to dance on it. He danced for awhile, and then he bent down to listen. "Nothing," he said, throwing up his hands. "I hear nothing."

"Well, all right," said the first bad boy. The two bad boys walked around the edge of the graveyard together. It was starting to get dark. They had windbreaker jackets tied around their waists, and now they untied the windbreakers and put them on to guard against the October chill.

"You know," said the first bad boy after awhile. "I've also heard that if you put a bare foot on a person's grave and stand really still, you can feel the heat being generated by the dead person's body."

"You've got to be kidding," said the second bad boy. "Want me to try that, too?"

"Sure," said the first bad boy, and he shrugged. But he was really a little bit afraid. It was now quite dark, and he didn't like the thought of having to put a bare foot on a person's grave. He was glad he wasn't going to be the one to try it.

The second bad boy took off one of his shoes and put it down into the dirt on top of one of the graves. He stood still for a minute, trying to see if he could feel the heat from the dead body. "I don't feel a thing!" he shouted to the first bad boy. But in fact he was sweating like crazy and could feel his own heartbeat. There was something terribly unnerving about standing on a grave with a bare foot, in near-darkness.

"Hey there!" the boys suddenly heard. It was the cemetery's night watchman speaking. "What do you think you're doing out here so late?"

"Nothing," said the boys.

"Don't you know how disrespectful it is to stand on people's graves like that? How do you think the relatives of these people would feel? Aren't you afraid the dead people here might curse you? Now get out of here before I call the police."

The bad boys ran away.

But not very far. They sat down on a bench outside the cemetery, where the night watchman couldn't see them.

"I don't care about being disrespectful," said the first bad boy. "It's only dead people."

"I don't care, either," said the second bad boy. "I'm not afraid at all."

"Really?" said the first bad boy. "Because I've got one more thing for us to try. I've heard that if you stick a knife way into a grave, the person in grave will reach out and grab you and you'll never be able to move from that spot until you die."

"Ridiculous!" said the second bad boy. But he was a little worried. "Too bad we don't have knives on us, or we could try it out."

"Actually," said the first bad boy. "I brought two knives with me. See?"

"I'm only going to try this if you try it, too," said the second bad boy.

"It's a deal," said the first.

It was now so dark out that the two bad boys couldn't even see the hands in front of their faces, so they knew that the night watchman had no chance of spotting them sneaking back into the cemetery.

They walked very carefully, as they couldn't quite see where they were going. But before long the second bad boy bumped into a headstone, and the two of them squatted on the ground and took out the knifes.

"Now!" they said, in unison, and plunged the knives into the grave.

Feeling nothing, they started to laugh. They both began to stand up. But then they realized that something was holding them to the grave. Neither could stand up or move away. "Help!" they shrieked. "Help!!!" They were horrified, and screamed and screamed for help at the top of their lungs.

But the night watchman was listening to a concert on his walkman, and he didn't hear their cries.

The next morning the cemetery's daytime watchman, checking the grounds, came across an awful sight. Both boys lay dead upon the grave, their mouths open in terror. It had been so dark that they'd accidentally pinned each other's jacket to the surface of the grave with their knives, and they had died of sheer fright.

Cards and the Founding of the United States of America

When all those European explorers like Columbus started popping in on the Americas, it took a looooooonnnnnnggggg time for their boats to get from there to here. Among all the things all those tightly quartered men did was 1) smell real bad, and 2) play lots of cards.

The popularity of cards continued as the colonies matured toward an independent nation. Thomas Jefferson played cards to relax while he was writing the Declaration of Independence, and George Washington loved to play cards so much that he kept a record of his card-playing achievements in his diary. And old Benjamin Franklin, among his many achievements, printed and sold playing cards.

When Americans like Ben Franklin, quite proud of their newly secured independence, first started printing their own playing cards, they were determined to have nothing to do with awful Kings and Queens. So other figures were substituted. George Washington was "President of Hearts." John Adams was the King of Diamonds, and Ben Franklin and Lafayette replaced the Clubs and Spades. Once the new nation gained a bit of self-confidence, printers turned away from such excessive and symbolic patriotic paranoia.

During the Civil War, however, card decks once again suddenly turned patriotic. Instead of Kings,

A deck of Bambi: Some of the earliest cards in America were made from the skins of sheep and deer!

there were generals; goddesses of liberty were substituted for Queens; and artillery officers took the place of Jacks. And instead of Hearts, Diamonds, Spades, and Clubs, there were flags, stars, military shields, and American eagles.

Today, in a time of efficient, international travel (unlike our ancestors, we can get across the ocean without smelling too bad) consider how great a deck of playing cards is for travel. A deck of cards is familiar to people all over the world (while some fancy languages like French or Portuguese are not). So playing cards is something you can do almost wherever you go.

The Joker

The Jokers are those two extra cards that come with a deck and seemingly serve no purpose. The Joker is usually pictured as some silly guy dressed up in some goofy way that would get any normal kid kicked out of school.

Now get a load of this: card historians claim that Jokers became part of the regular deck during the 1860s because of euchre, a game that needed a deck with an extra card, and that, eventually, people kept misspelling the word "euchre" until it became the word "joker."

GIVE US A BREAK!!!

Just what kind of spellers were these Americans in the 1860s?! Euchre becomes joker?! Jerker or dorker would be much easier to believe.

This explanation is like saying Dexter comes from the once-successful book publisher Fred, and that throughout the mid-1990s, the word Fred was just sort of misspelled into Dexter.

Our Favorite
Palindromes

(a word or sentence that reads the same backward as forward)

Madam, I'm Adam.

Step on no pets.

May a moody baby doom a yam?

Lewd did I live, & evil I did dwel.

A man, a plan, a canal—Panama!

Doc, note, I dissent. A fast never prevents a fatness. I diet on cod.

Never odd or even.

Dennis, Nell, Edna, Leon, Nedra, Anita, Rolf, Nora, Alice, Carol, Leo, Jane, Reed, Dena, Dale, Basil, Rae, Penny, Lana, Dave, Denny, Lena, Ida, Bernadette, Ben, Ray, Lila, Nina, Jo, Ira, Mara, Sara, Mario, Jan, Ina, Lily, Arne, Bette, Dan, Reba, Diane, Lynn, Ed, Eva, Dana, Lynne, Pearl, Isabel, Ada, Ned, Dee, Rena, Joel, Lora, Cecil, Aaron, Flora, Tina, Arden, Noel, and Ellen sinned.

Sit on a potato pan, Otis.

The lights you see when you close your eyes real hard are called *phosphenes.*

Hairy
Fairy Tales

Have you ever noticed that fairy tales seem to be a little obsessed with hair? There's Goldilocks, whose hair was apparently so striking that no one remembered to give her a normal name. There's Snow White, with her "Hair as black as ebony." There are The Three Little Pigs, who were always talking about the hair on their chinny chin chins. And, of course, there's Rapunzel, whose hair grew to such lengths that she could lower it out her window and have princes and witches climbing up it as if it were an escalator.

If Rapunzel were alive today, actually, she'd be in the Guinness Book of World Records for sure. The facts is, most of us couldn't grow more than three feet of hair, even if we stayed away from the beauty shop and barber for the rest of our lives. Our hair keeps growing, sure, but at a certain point the strands reach a maximum length, rest at that length, and then fall out. Very few people have a maximum length of longer than three feet.

Here's another reason to wonder about Rapunzel: How could she have grown so much hair at such a young age? Hair only grows about six inches a year. Is there something wrong with Rapunzel? Should she consult a qualified physician?

Top 10
(and one other)
Dog Names

1	Brandy
2	Lady
3	Max
4	Rocky
5	Sam
6	Heidi
7	Sheba
8	Ginger
9	Muffin
10	Bear
24,385	Planet Dexter

Last Words

"*Haircut!*"
—Albert Anastasia, gangster, shot while in a barber's chair

"*This wallpaper is killing me; one of us has got to go.*"
—Oscar Wilde, playwright

"*It's very beautiful over there.*"
—Thomas Edison, inventor

"*Why, yes—a bullet-proof vest.*"
—James W. Rodgers, murderer executed by a firing squad, when asked if he had a final request

"*They couldn't hit an elephant at this dist—*"
—John Sedgwick, Civil War general, carelessly looking over the battlefield

"*One day when the going is tough and a big game is hanging in the balance, ask the team to win one for the Gipper. I don't know where I'll be, Rock, but I'll know about it, and I'll be happy.*"
—George Gipp, football star, his last request to coach Knute Rockne

Supercalifragilisticexpialidocious, from the movie *Mary Poppins* means "good."

"So little done. So much to do!"
—Alexander Graham Bell, inventor

"Hullo."
—Rupert Brooke, poet

"Dying is a very dull, dreary affair. And my advice to you is to have nothing whatever to do with it."
—W. Somerset Maugham, writer

"Why should I talk to you? I've just been talking to your boss."
—Wilson Mizner, Hollywood impresario, to an attendant priest

"Wish you were here—instead of me!"
—Richard Halliburton, explorer, final signal sent from his sinking ship

"Good-bye, everybody!"
—Hart Crane, poet, jumping off ship

"Die, my dear doctor? That's the last thing I shall do."
—Viscount Henry John Temple Palmerston, statesman

"On the contrary."
—Henrik Ibsen, dramatist, to his wife who said he was looking better

"Oh, Mother, how beautiful it is."
—Maury Paul, gossip columnist

"Last words are for fools who haven't said enough."
—Karl Marx, Communist

Exiting . . . with a Smile
(Actual Epitaphs)

Epitaph (EP-ih-taf) n. An inscription on a tombstone in memory of the one buried there.

• •

School is out
Teacher
Has gone home
—for a professor;
    Elkhart, Indiana

Here Lies
John Yeast
Pardon Me
For Not Rising
—Ruidoso, New Mexico

Once I wasn't
Then I was
Now I ain't
Again
—Lee County, Mississippi

Underneath this pile of
    stones
Lies all that's left of Sally
    Jones.
Her name was Briggs, it
    was not Jones,
But Jones was used to
    rhyme with stones.
—Skaneateles, New York

This is on me . . .
—Rhode Island

America's first pizzeria opened in New York City in 1895.

Here lies
    Lester Moore
Four slugs
from a 44
no Les
no more
—Tombstone,
Arizona

Fear God, Keep the
    commandments,
    and
Don't attempt to climb
    a tree,
For that's what caused the
    death of me.
        —Kent, England

Here lies Jane Smith, wife
of Thomas Smith, marble
cutter. This monument was
erected by her husband as a
tribute to her memory and a
specimen of his work.
Monuments of the same
style 350 dollars.
        —Springdale, Ohio

In memory of
Mrs. Alpha White
Weight 309 lbs
Open wide ye heavenly gates
That lead to the heavenly
    shore;
Our father suffered in pass-
    ing through
And mother weighs much
    more.
        —Lee, Massachusetts

Stranger, approach this
    spot with gravity.
John Brown is filling his
    last cavity.
        —for a dentist

More?

Even More Planet Dexter Books!
● ● ●

Look for these in your favorite book or toy store. If they don't carry them, they can always order them so you'll have them within 48 hours to a week.

Grossology
The Science of Really Gross Things!
by Sylvia Branzei

Instant Creature
The Swimming Critters from Way Back Then
(includes eggs and food! just add water! instant life!)
by The Editors of Planet Dexter

The Hairy Book
The (Uncut) Truth About the Weirdness of Hair
by The Editors of Planet Dexter

Animal Grossology
The Science of Creatures Gross and Disgusting
by Sylvia Branzei

Planet Ant
(includes Ant Planet & ants-by-mail coupon!)
by The Editors of Planet Dexter